Easy Does It Relationship Guide

Easy Does It Relationship Guide

For People in Recovery

Mary Faulkner

Hazelden
Center City, Minnesota 55012-0176
1-800-328-0094
1-651-213-4590 (Fax)
www.hazelden.org

Library of Congress Cataloging-in-Publication Data

Faulkner, Mary, M.A.
    Easy does it relationship guide : for people in recovery /
    Mary Faulkner
    p. cm.
    Includes bibliographical references and index.
    ISBN 978-1-59285-352-6
    1. Recovering addicts—Psychology. 2. Interpersonal
    relations. I. Title.

HV 4998.F38 2007
646.70087'4—dc22

                                                2006048019

11 10 09 08 07   6 5 4 3 2 1

Editor's Note:
The stories in this book are based on the author's discussions with
recovering couples in focus groups. Names and details have been
changed to protect anonymity.

Cover design by Theresa Gedig
Interior design by Rachel Holscher
Typesetting by Prism Publishing Center

Contents

Gratitude

I want to thank the couples who participated in the focus groups and those who organized and hosted these get-togethers. Thanks to the staff at Hazelden, particularly Karen Chernyaev for her excellent editing. A special thanks to my agent, Linda Roghaar, and a great big appreciation to Norma Wimberly for her constant reminder—*Pause when agitated*—which reverberates in my head and throughout this book. A special thanks to friend Norm Woodel for his steak grilling skills as well as the careful listening and good suggestions that sharpened the text. And as always, thanks to all whose work fed my thoughts and helped bring this book into being.

Author's Note on Exercises

Twelve Step meeting protocol is recommended for the partner exercises included throughout this book. Respect each other's viewpoints and beliefs. Listen; don't question or critique. Avoid interrupting or getting into your own story until it's your turn. Agree to turn off phones in advance. Practice confidentiality. Don't call your best friend afterward and share details of the intimate conversation, and don't bring up the discussion again with your partner when the session is over. Set time limits around your sessions, and if your partner wants to talk further, set a time and place to do that. If either partner is tired or overwhelmed, table the discussion, but be sure to reschedule it. You're not trying to fix each other; you're telling your story by exploring the deep beliefs and attitudes that have been part of your formation. Healing doesn't depend on resolving differences; it comes through accepting them—with sensitivity.

The exercises in this book are designed to facilitate a focused discussion between partners, and they are most helpful when used this way. Partners can do them individually, but the point is to learn more about each other, deepen understanding, and build trust—a goal best achieved by working together.

"We Shall Intuitively Know . . ."

It might seem like a stretch of the imagination to say that our desire for relationship began more than five hundred generations ago—but it's not entirely untrue. Since the dawn of history, we have been encoded with the yearning to form a relationship and make a home with another person. The basic urge to jump the broom, or make some other declaration of *togethering*, is strong, regardless of the trail of broken dreams in our rearview mirror. Consider our willingness to try one more time to make a go of it, in spite of our past difficulties. Something inside us says yes to that primordial urge to go out there and give love our best shot, despite the fear and misgivings. What prompts us to follow the stirring of the heart and to make another lover's leap?

Call this yearning the human spirit, instinct, or the prodding of a Higher Power. In recovery we are drawn forward into life. We may think we didn't get a map, yet we all have intuition, an internal, onboard navigation system to guide us on that sometimes uneasy mission of fully realizing who and what we are. Think of it as a GPS—a God Positioning System. Nowhere is there a greater place to evolve, to learn about self, and to practice recovery principles than in relationship, either with child, friend, spouse, or parent. The focus here is on relationship with what's known as a significant other—spouse, mate, lover, life partner, whatever term best fits us.

This book is a sequel to the *Easy Does It Dating Guide*, which takes readers through a process of clean-and-sober dating, including making a commitment to a lasting relationship. The *Easy Does It Relationship Guide* was born out of the question, "Now that I have one, what do I do with it?" This book offers suggestions on how to attain, maintain, and sustain a satisfying committed relationship while remaining clean and sober. It applies Twelve Step principles to the relationship and includes the hope, strength, and experiences of other recovering couples. The stories here—with names and details changed—are based on meetings with recovering couples throughout the United States. They present a picture of the real-life struggles of partners in committed relationships who are working Twelve Step recovery programs. In some instances, both partners are recovering from substance abuse. In others, one partner is in recovery from addiction and the other is in Al-Anon, an organization for friends, family, and others close to substance abusers. Relationship durations ranged from less than a year to more than twenty. Regardless of the kind of addiction, the length of the relationship, or the region of the country, the challenges couple spoke about were surprisingly similar.

This book presents helpful information along with suggestions and exercises for strengthening relational skills, including how to have a fair fight. It helps readers find resolution with the past and create a vision for a shared future that expresses their love as well as their hopes and dreams. And it does this while keeping the emphasis on recovery.

Chapter One *

What Does a Healthy Relationship Look Like?

In attempting to achieve a healthy relationship it's helpful to know what one looks like, but that's not always possible. Many of us don't have role models and aren't sure what we're trying to do. We're making it up as we go—we're winging it. And in fact there's no universal definition of a healthy relationship, no master plan. It's what we and our partner want it to be, and that keeps unfolding as we go. As a starting point and to keep it simple, let's say a healthy relationship is a *recovering* relationship. It's based on Twelve Step principles. Recovering relationships are living organisms. They grow and change along with the people in them, and as such they're acts of faith.

Couples in long-term relationships talk about celebrating good times, enjoying the quieter times, and enduring the tough times. They say a satisfying friendship, the warmth of companionship, a wealth of meaningful memories, and a sense of having successfully navigated some of life's greatest challenges have rewarded them. No one says it's easy, but their commitment to each other, to the relationship, and to recovery deepens. They stay because they want to.

So where do we find these couples?

One couple had driven sixty miles from their small town in Minnesota to attend our focus group in St. Paul. They talked about their twenty-seven-year relationship, in which they have weathered active addiction, recovery, a partner's relapse, and a divorce. They gave themselves a second chance at recovery and marriage and are well into round two. They both said their commitment to the program comes first in their marriage. They know from experience that if they lose their recovery, they stand to lose it all.

A Seattle couple is still struggling with one partner's active addiction. They value their fifteen-year marriage, and their commitment to stay together is strong. They are temporarily living apart for the children's sake, but they haven't given up on their miracle. They hope and pray that recovery will make it possible for them to get back together under one roof again.

A couple in Boston is taking their marriage one day at a time while they both work an Al-Anon program. They are committed to personal growth and learning new skills. Their commitment to each other runs deep. They've known each other since they were kids.

A couple in Memphis suffered the terrible heartbreak of a child's death, unpayable medical bills, and bankruptcy. They talked about powerlessness and gratitude in the midst of grief. They've learned the value of stepping back, prioritizing, and *letting go*. They've stayed sober and stayed together through very tough times, saying that while they don't always feel good they do feel stronger. Seven years after the loss of their child, the grief comes in waves. "We take turns being strong and collapsing under the burden of it," Sally said. "There have been good times along the way, too, and we've learned to enjoy them but not try to hang on to them."

A recovering alcoholic in Chicago is making his third attempt at a committed relationship—the first in sobriety. Tom was embarrassed to admit being overwhelmed at the difficulty of partnering. He felt that after two previous marriages, he shouldn't be surprised, but he was. "I drank through my first two marriages, so this is almost like a first try. If I knew how hard this was going to be, I'm not sure I would have taken it on. That is in no way a negative comment on Laura. I love her with all my heart and have no desire to leave the marriage—it's just difficult." Laura attends Al-Anon regularly and agreed with her partner, saying marriage is challenging but not as difficult for her as it is for Tom. At least for now, she added, smiling. They find support in Recovering Couples Anonymous.

Words like *enduring, commitment*, and the *long haul* may sound daunting. But in relationships as in recovery, we don't have to know how to do it all before we begin, and it doesn't all happen on the first day.

But What Does It Look Like?

Creating a healthy relationship could be compared to sculpting the proverbial elephant: we chip away everything that isn't an elephant. There's truth in that old joke. Isn't that what we do in recovery? All those searching and fearless inventories and other self-reflections are a process of chipping away the stuff that isn't who we really are. Our perfect relationship, like recovery, is a work in progress.

In the big picture, a healthy relationship is one in which both partners are more satisfied than dissatisfied, and actively strive to increase that positive ratio. In the small picture, it depends on both partners' abilities to meet their own basic needs and experience satisfaction.

The Serenity Prayer gives us further clues. *God grant me the serenity to accept the things I cannot change, the courage to change the things I can, and the wisdom to know the difference.* We might say that a healthy relationship is a study in wisdom, as it is surely an exercise in acceptance and change. We strive to find harmony in our differences, to accept one another and the way the relationship is going at any given moment. Yet human relationships are always changing.

In healthy relationships, couples learn to hold it all lightly—to embrace conflict, resolve differences, and seek serenity. When they find it, they enjoy it. When it slips away again, as it does, they have the tools to regain it. Each partner is *involved* in the process. Involvement needs *honesty.* There is no place for manipulation, trauma-drama, controlling, or dropping out. Resolving differences isn't done by winning or losing a disagreement but by coming to a new position—one in which both individuals learn something new about themselves and each other, and in some way embrace a new idea, attitude, or behavior. For that to happen we have to maintain our integrity, upholding an honest difference of opinion, expressing sincere emotional reactions and responses—*living in our truth.*

Life on Life's Terms

A healthy relationship is free to look bad. There are situations that no amount of "We're fine" can cover. Hard times don't necessarily indicate an unhealthy partnership. On the contrary, life dishes out some tough stuff. Partners rely on each other for support as they face life on life's terms. And there are times when it's a partner who is dishing out the tough stuff. In healthy partnerships we can carry one another, at least for a time. Often it is the belief we have in each other that turns things around. There are unlimited possibilities besides hanging on for dear life or leaving. Mates in healthy relationships explore that territory together at meetings, with sponsors, or through counseling. They look for options and make conscious choices.

Partnership is about relating, with the emphasis on *ing*. It's an action. Having a healthy relationship is a matter of taking the necessary steps to make it happen. It isn't different from any other aspect of our recovery program. Recovery isn't just about not taking a drink or not engaging in whatever addiction or compulsion was our nemeses. It requires consistently showing up and doing the work: willingness. A healthy relationship works the same way. We show up, willing to chisel away at our self-imposed limits, and we have the potential to transcend—to grow and become more in the process.

Even Carrots Need Tending

Growing a relationship is like raising a carrot crop—both need tending. An obvious benefit to growing carrots and cultivating a relationship is that both feed us. We till the soil, plant the seeds, pull the weeds, and eventually reap the benefits. A healthy relationship reflects our willingness to do the work and nurture the seeds. Love grows, but left untended it can also wither and die. In successful relationships, partners speak the words of love and show their devotion generously and often. Making love is one of the ways we reinforce our bonds—it is the culmination of affection, gentle thoughts, little acts of kindness, and the passion we feel for life.

LIVING WITH SPIRIT

It's been said that relationships are threesomes—two partners and the relationship itself. For recovering relationships we might want to add a fourth member to the organization—a Higher Power. How we identify our spiritual source and how we honor that part of our partnership is personal. But relying on a Higher Power is very likely going to make a difference in our capacity to experience satisfaction in our relationships. A relationship between two satisfied people can't help but become a wellspring of contentment—enough for the partners and a generous overflow. We may have had the experience of being in the company of a couple who have it going together. It splashes out everywhere, and it feels good.

In this book, you'll meet couples nationwide who describe the spirit of their relationship in a variety of ways. They talk about acceptance, appreciation, and praise; presence and availability; empathy and compassion; good lovemaking; playfulness and joy; endurance, steadfastness, freedom, and willingness. Perhaps most important, a healthy relationship is made of the bodies, minds, and spirits of two people spiritually connected. It is *Higher Powered*.

The following exercises will help you discern what you both want to create in your relationship—to identify the special character or spirit of your partnership.

EXERCISES

Taking Stock

Work together and identify the qualities you want in your relationship. Don't list what you don't want—state the items in positive terms. For example, if you don't want to feel confined, perhaps you want a sense of *freedom, openness,* or *room to be.*

Next, make a list of the qualities you *have* in your relationship. Again, stay with positive qualities. This can give you a sense of what you've already accomplished and where you may want to focus.

Finding Your Vision

From the lists you've just made, begin to identify a vision together for the relationship. Conscious awareness of what we hope to accomplish together lifts us out of the everyday annoyances that can turn into problems. It gets us operating from a higher place.

In designing your vision statement, include how you make decisions and solve problems. Again, state items in positive terms: for example, *This is a relationship where we share problems and work out solutions together.* Visions can be big enough to encompass the hopes and dreams of each partner—even when they don't appear to match. For example, I met a couple who found that one partner's desire to "nest" at home seemed to clash with the other's longing for high adventure and faraway places. They came up with the following vision: *This is a home where everyone's dreams can come true.* There's no doubt they will work through their differences creatively. When times get rough and it seems you're at an impasse, go back to your vision statement and read it together—you'll be surprised at how it helps you refocus on higher goals.

As you read this book, pay attention to the information and suggestions that offer further insight into your vision and the exercises that help you reach where you want to be.

* * *

Remember, a healthy relationship is something partners create together; it reflects their spirit and the spirit of recovery—it's Higher Powered. Our relationship grows and changes as we grow and change; it's a living organism. Many recovering couples say that on good days they have most of the following qualities: satisfaction, acceptance, growth and change, curiosity, a spirit of service, honesty, involvement, conflict and resolution, truth, and serenity. On "bad" days they have at least a few of them.

Next we'll gain some insight into family patterns and how they influence our present commitments.

Chapter Two *

How We Got Here

Addiction disconnected our system. Recovery is a process of reconnecting and rewiring as needed. It's an opportunity to sort through the messages we've heard about life, what we've been told about ourselves, and what we've discovered on our own. We can choose what is most true for us at this time in our lives, particularly regarding relationships.

First Things First: What *Is* Commitment, Anyway?

Any discussion of relationship in the recovering community quickly runs into that "C-word," *commitment,* a word often confused with the sound of a cell door slamming. We might hear it as a life sentence. Previous bad experiences, fear of failure, and sometimes just facing the unknown make us apprehensive. Some say commitment has been co-opted by contemporary culture—it's become more about society's needs than ours. Commitment becomes entangled with issues such as taxes and medical benefits, child support, prenuptial agreements, marriage vows, domestic partnerships, and civil unions. With all the paperwork, it's lost its connection to the heart—to love. Laws and legal documents exist for the benefit of each individual partner, and it is important for partners to get the details down. But that's not the purpose of this book; this book is about the *spirit* in which couples come together and about how to keep it alive.

Recovery begins with a commitment we make to ourselves—a conscious decision to live a clean and sober life and grow spiritually. We don't know at the time exactly what that will mean. In a committed relationship, it's a decision made between two people, a promise representing the desire to be together and to face life as a team. And that is likewise full of twists and turns. We don't know what lies ahead. We're not supposed to know. Our elders were onto something when they included "for better or for worse" in the familiar wedding vows, because life together will include both. Couples are essentially committing to work through the difficulties—to live, love, and grow together. A friend of mine said it this way: "Commitment is signing on the dotted line, but it's lived in the small print."

Today not all committed relationships include marriage, and not all marriages include traditional wedding vows. Some who are reading this book are already in relationships and marriages. Others may be contemplating taking this step. Regardless of where we are in the process, this is a chance to clarify what we are doing—to talk about what we're building. Commitment isn't something imposed from the outside—it's something discovered within. Recovery has given us the freedom to design a life that works for us. Recovering partnerships give us the freedom to design a life together that works for each of us.

THE ESSENTIAL QUESTION: WHO AM I?

Recovery is a spiritual journey, and many say that journey is driven by one essential question: Who am I? The search takes us back to our origins and explores family issues as a way of better understanding ourselves today. Our commitment story begins there. Understanding our family relationships, how they worked, and their effects on us ultimately frees us to be in the one we're in now—informed by the past, but free of its power over us.

Where we were born—the part of the world, the town, even the neighborhood—contributes to the making of who we are. Religion, education, and media can have a big influence on learning and behavior, but our family has the most immediate hand in shaping us and in giving us our basic beliefs. By the time we walk out the door for kindergarten, we are budding young social scientists, politicians, and mood managers. Understanding how *our* family works shapes how we believe families are *supposed* to work—and how we expect the world to work. What it takes to get a parent to smile influences how we make others smile. All of this is wired into place—below the level of consciousness.

Family of origin is the modern-day version of the tribe, and family rules carry the power of tribal law. For the rest of our lives we weigh and measure people, places, and things against this system—until we bump into someone from a different tribe and our beliefs are called into question. We may have already discovered that while we heard the same mating call our partner did, we have very different ways of responding to it. The good news is that successful relationships are about exploring differences. And while instincts don't change, tribal beliefs can, and do. Examining them is part of the business of growing up.

Sorting through the family beliefs we grew up with and claiming the thoughts, feelings, and values that are really ours: this is a process of taking responsibility. It is spiritual maturity. In recovery this process of discernment begins with Step work and goes on throughout life: that's what it means to gain self-awareness and to grow spiritually.

That "Road of Happy Destiny"

Long-term partnerships don't just happen. They are the result of growing together, developing new attitudes, and learning new skills. Despite a sincere desire to make a lasting commitment, we sometimes unconsciously undermine our success. More often than not this is due to unfinished family-of-origin issues.

Therapist and author John Bradshaw revolutionized the recovering community with his profoundly simple revelation that in healthy families you are allowed to grow up and leave. Children who are raised in healthy families develop the life skills necessary for successful relationships. They grow up knowing what it feels like to count on others and to be counted on—to belong. A necessary process of bonding and trusting occurs. They will leave home confident, curious, and ready to engage life. They know how to be friends, team members, co-workers, and neighbors—and when the time comes they have what it takes to make a commitment to a partner and to be in a healthy relationship. That's the ideal. But for a variety of reasons it doesn't happen that way for many of us who are in recovery from addiction and the cluster of accompanying conditions.

Many times, through no one's direct fault, stressful situations take parental attention away from children. It can be due to the immaturity of parents, demanding careers, illness, addiction in the home, death of a spouse, or other life challenges. When kids don't get what they need, when they don't get the kind of care necessary to develop the qualities they'll need in life, their instruction book is a few chapters short. Most significantly, they are short on trust. This unfinished family business interferes with the ability to bond with a partner—that's what Bradshaw means by *leaving home*. Regardless, nature moves us along on our path, ready or not! When it's time to fly the nest and follow the mating call, most of us respond to it with or without the full set of instructions.

The Family Saga

Therapist and author Patrick Carnes talks about the family epoch. The word is apt, because the dynamic contains conditioning acquired over many generations. Family history continues to determine our fate until we unravel it—*and rewrite it*. When we don't clear family-of-origin issues, we replay them in some way with a family of our own. We want to commit to a partner, but it feels overwhelming. That sense of obligation to our old family is like a huge debt with high interest. We keep paying but it doesn't go away.

The exercises in this chapter will help you explore your family history. Before you begin, consider these general suggestions:

1. Set boundaries as part of writing your new story. Old behaviors cannot be extinguished and reinforced at the same time. It might be necessary to limit interactions with our family of origin while we make the changes.
2. Find other couples who have what we want and notice what they do and how they do it; this provides models while we design our own version of

a healthy relationship. Consider finding a marriage sponsor. Investigate Recovering Couples Anonymous.

3. In recovery we strive to live by spiritual principles, not necessarily by the family rules we grew up with. This allows us to transcend the past, letting go of old thoughts and thinking new ones. Applying spiritual principles to life is the up-to-the-minute instruction book we've been looking for.

Exercises

These exercises can help you and your partner explore each other's belief systems around relationship. Knowing where behavior (ours or our partner's) is coming from doesn't eliminate all the arguments but, at the very least, goes a long way toward damage control.

Exploring Beliefs

- What are three beliefs you learned in your family of origin that are important to you?
- What are three beliefs you now have that differ from your family of origin's beliefs?
- Where did your "different" beliefs come from?

Exploring Attitudes

- What are three basic attitudes your family of origin has about life?
- What attitudes do you now have about life that differ from theirs?
- How did you develop your particular attitudes?
- If you were to make an attitude adjustment, where would you start?

Exploring Values
- What are three values you learned at home?
- Who taught them to you?
- What values do you have that differ from your family's values?
- Where did they come from?

Exploring Trust
- Who took care of you as a child?
- What kind of discipline was used in your family of origin?
- What kind of praise did you receive?
- What did you need to hear?

Revitalizing Your Promises
Using that material, talk about the new story: what you want in your life together. What are you creating? Brainstorm a positive behavior that takes you one step further into your new story and commit to doing it.

* * *

We have an instinct to bond with our "tribe" and another instinct that nudges us to leave home and bond with a mate. These instincts are shaped by culture—primarily family. Bonding happens as we are nurtured in infancy and childhood by parents or other primary caretakers who are emotionally present. The trust that is learned there allows us to make a commitment with a partner. Recovery holds the key for healing broken trust and for successful relating. Updating our system, role modeling, and making positive changes provide the best chance for successful partnering.

Next we'll look at another equally intriguing and sometimes hair-raising aspect of relationship—intimacy, that other "C-word."

Chapter Three *

Intimacy: The Other "C-Word"

Intimacy possibly runs a close second to commitment in the "most terrifying concept" category, giving it the status of that other C-word, even though it clearly begins with an I. Often the word *intimacy* is used to refer to sex, but this chapter focuses on the emotional, mental, and spiritual nature of intimacy. Its sexual nature is discussed in chapter 8.

Someone came up with the helpful way of describing intimacy: "in-to-me-see." It begins with self-awareness: becoming conscious of our thoughts, feelings, and emotions— our reality—and sharing these insights with our partner. Intimacy isn't something we get from a relationship, it is something we bring to it.

Intimacy deepens as trust grows. We increasingly risk sharing personal "stuff" that we might not talk about with other people, such as fears, insecurities, and disappointments, as well as hopes and dreams. Intimacy depends on a good feedback loop: I tell you something about me and you tell me something about you. We'll continue disclosing to the degree that our story is met with genuine interest and sensitivity—in a word, acceptance.

Intimacy doesn't only happen between partners. We can be intimate with friends and family, and there are moments of personal intimacy when we relax and experience just *being*. Such times are important to our serenity. Spending time in nature, digging in the garden, fishing in a favorite stream, puttering in the garage, even cuddling up in a chair with the cat are intimacies: they are important interludes that strengthen our connection to self and nurture our spirit. Healthy partnering doesn't exclude these other intimacies but rather is fed by them. Relying exclusively on each other for all our intimacy needs overburdens the relationship. Enjoying friendships and activities and continuing to pursue our interests keeps us true to the commitment to grow in self-awareness—it ensures that our life together stays vibrant.

Intimacy becomes a living, breathing bond between partners as they share experiences. Sharing doesn't necessarily imply doing everything together—it includes sharing new insights and awarenesses gained through these experiences. Again, a partnership gains life as each partner moves through a personal process—living, learning, growing, and changing. This *growing, changing* quality adds to intimacy's mysterious nature. "More shall be revealed" is a saying in recovery. This goes double for a relationship.

The Plane to Flagstaff

Several years ago I signed up for the adventure of a lifetime—a trip through the Grand Canyon on the Colorado River with three other women. After making the decision to go, we began making plans. We got books, maps, pictures, grilled the rafting company staff extensively, and talked with others who had taken this trip. We took our gear list to an outfitter and bought the right clothes, sleeping bags, tents, flashlights, and everything else that was suggested. We trained, hiked, and worked out at the gym. The day finally arrived, and we drove to the airport and boarded the plane to Flagstaff, Arizona, our jumping-off point. We had done everything we could to prepare, but from that moment on, the adventure took over. It was out of our hands—*we lost control of it.*

I remember what our trip leader said as he passed around a document that we signed to release the company from any personal injury claims. He told us, "Look at the river. Now look at the canyon walls. You're in the wilderness—there aren't any sidewalks, no traffic lights, no 'watch your step' signs. Others have taken this trip, but our journey will be unique. We don't know exactly what lies ahead. The river moves constantly, and the scenery changes every day. Weather blows through this canyon in fast and unpredictable ways." He told us we were now an *expedition.* That the safety and security of the group depended on each of us paying attention and following a few safety rules, which he explained. He concluded by saying, "You're on your own, but we're in this thing together."

He was right. Each day brought exciting new experiences. In the time we spent together in the canyon each of us hit some kind of personal limit. We each encountered fears and insecurities we didn't realize we had, and we each had to reach out to the others to get through it. We all had a turn wishing we hadn't attempted such a rigorous vacation, and in our own way made that familiar promise "If I ever get out of here . . . " However, we made it: we finished the trip, and eventually we were all richer for the experience.

It occurs to me that intimacy in a committed relationship is like that Grand Canyon experience. We are an *expedition*— responsible for ourselves and "in it together" at the same time. We move through life, and the internal landscape is always changing—we are constantly encountering new and different aspects of ourselves. We'll be challenged beyond our capacity, we'll have meltdowns, and we'll have to depend on each other. In the course of events we'll witness the best and worst in each other. But at the end of each day, we'll crawl into the tent together, and the next morning we'll get up and go again. Life is an adventure, recovery is an adventure, and your relationship is one, too. Adventures don't come without risk and neither do relationships. Of all the aspects of a relationship, intimacy is the most risky.

Intimacy: Authentically You

In the course of a lifetime we cast ourselves in many roles. We are students, employees, co-workers, politicians, plumbers, and teachers. Each role is like a part in a play. We improvise a bit and put our mark on it to a degree, but for the most part we are bound by the script.

In an intimate relationship we step out of the roles, put down the script, and respond to a partner in the moment, from our heart. Such vulnerability carries risk. Disclosure includes surprises. We realize things we'd rather not know about ourselves—and we risk discovering things about our mate that make us wonder if we've made a mistake. Intimacy is about getting real together, and reality includes the whole package. There is that inevitable moment when we look across the breakfast table and fear we have married our lover's evil twin! Success depends on being comfortable enough with ourself to get uncomfortable with someone else—daring to hang in there and work through the challenges together.

There's a higher risk factor with intimacy when abuse or

childhood trauma is part of our story. As noted earlier, if we've grown up in a home where it wasn't safe to trust, healing has to happen. Gradually, by sharing our stories at safe levels, we get more comfortable. Intimacy grows as healing progresses and vice versa. There are times when childhood wounds can be too intense for the relationship; partners can feel overwhelmed by their own or their mate's injuries. Honesty calls for admitting what we can't handle and finding further help.

Why Do We Do It?

Given the apparent hugeness of the endeavor, the high stakes, why do we do this intimacy thing? Why do we lay ourselves on the line like that? The answer is deceptively simple: we *need* to be known and to know another. The soul cannot see itself; it is reflected back to us through our intimate encounters. The closer we get with another person, the deeper into ourselves we go. This is both the hunger for intimacy and the fear of it. We long to be known and loved, but at the same time we fear we will be found unbearably inadequate, hopelessly flawed—unlovable in some terrible way. And what we fear is true: beauty and the beast coexist in each of us.

We are human, imperfect, and incapable of perfect love. There is that chance that our partner will be driven away by our beast, but it's more likely that we will drive our partner away by our own fear of it—*our inability to love ourself.* This is where reliance on a Higher Power is called for. We need a sense of unconditional love—something that transcends human frailty. Partners will always encounter qualities within each other that they don't, won't, or can't come to grips with. Impasses don't have to be deal-breakers. The principle of acceptance doesn't depend on liking a condition or situation, it means coming to a peaceful resolution with it. We can choose to not make it a big deal, agree to disagree, or "turn it over" and hope for the best. This isn't denial; it's survival. Ultimately we improve our ability to do this—to transcend ourselves—and the relationship grows richer for it.

Fearfully, yet courageously, we take the risk. We stick our toe into the water. As small revelations are met with acceptance, the heart opens and love grows. The depth of intimacy depends on our willingness to face the unknown: that which is inside us that we can know only through another person. In that way we become witnesses to each other's lives—partners on the spiritual adventure.

What to Expect

The difference between an adventure and an outing is that adventures lift us out of our routine. Sooner or later we take a chance and board the plane to Flagstaff. At the same time, having the right equipment improves our odds for a successful experience. The following suggestions can improve the chances for developing intimacy in our relationship, given that there aren't any formulas.

Boundaries

Personal boundaries are necessary for healthy intimacy. They allow us to stay in our center and still be close to someone. Boundaries keep us from either absorbing or disappearing into each other, or needing to put up walls. Healthy personal boundaries are flexible; they allow us to explore new territory while feeling safe. They give us the choice of letting someone in or keeping them out.

There is no rule that says we should tell each other everything we've ever done, every thought that crosses our mind, every fear and worry. We can use common sense. Learning to respect our own boundaries means listening to that little voice inside that says it's not ready to share that yet— making intimacy different from confession.

Awareness of Self and "Other"

We need to have a grasp on our own reality: knowing what we like, what we're feeling and thinking, and being aware that our partner has a different and equally important reality going on at the same time. Intimacy involves talking about these differences and learning from them.

Curiosity

Curiosity is opposite from "knowing it all" and from indifference. More than just being open to another's viewpoint, curiosity means seeking it, delighting in it, treasuring it. Through curiosity we discover what we most love about each other—our particular perspectives.

Honesty

Honesty is striving to live by our principles, saying what we mean and meaning what we say, but not dogmatically. We naturally grow and change; new understandings evolve with time. Honesty includes saying we don't know and changing our mind at times. Note, however, that persistent vagueness or avoidance raises questions about honesty. It can erode the necessary trust between partners.

Reachability

It may not appear in the dictionary, but *reachability* is used here to describe our willingness to let intimacy happen— without dogging it. We can desire intimacy, but if we are unreachable or overreaching it can't occur. Reachability includes healing patterns that keep us reacting to the past rather than being in the present moment. It means giving our relationship enough time and attention to flourish but not obsessing about it.

A Spirit of Forgiveness

With this spirit, we acknowledge that both parties are going to make mistakes, and both sides will need to forgive. Be quick to ask for forgiveness and generous in giving it when asked.

Openness to Influence

We allow ourself to be changed in our relationship. Influence means letting go of controlling patterns—both the need to be in control and the refusal to engage.

Remember the program acronym HOW, meaning *honest, open,* and *willing:* it can be a helpful description of what it takes to be intimate. It takes *honest* introspection, the *openness* to share our private thoughts and feelings with a partner, and the *willingness* to learn from each other.

INTIMACY: BETWEEN THE EXTREMES

It is rare for people in recovery to have all their emotional skills up and running. Our addiction often began as a way of self-medicating emotional pain. It worked for a while, but it slowed our progress. Healing takes however long it takes. As feelings begin waking up, they are overwhelming. For a while our emotions may seem black or white; it seems the only two options are *on* or *off*. Intimacy begins exploring the emotional territory in between these two extremes. At first it's a pretty narrow strip of ground. If your emotional vocabulary is limited to *good*, *bad*, or *fine*, refer to appendix A for an extensive cheat sheet. It helps to put names on the raw sensations.

If the idea of intimacy still feels scary, remember the laughter that happens at meetings as people connect to the feelings in each other's stories. It shows us that intimacy has its amusing moments. Humorist Steve Allen once said that comedy is tragedy plus time. There is only one rule to remember as you explore intimacy: respect everyone's feelings, including yours. For example, you might feel the lump in your throat when you think about sharing something very personal. This can be an indication that it isn't the right time or the right place. And other times you might feel "butterflies in your stomach," but you know it's time to move ahead anyway. Your intuition will guide you. Respect often means erring on the side of caution. Trust takes a long time to build, and it can be quickly undone.

Thinkers and Feelers

It's helpful to know that some of us perceive and express ourselves primarily through thought and others through emotion. It's both a matter of our personal nature and also what kind of expression the culture we grew up in valued. Intimacy for thinkers is more likely to be through sharing thoughts, plans, and ideas. To them, a meeting of the minds is where it's at. A thinker's emotional life is secondary to the thought process: the emotions are there, but they have less weight than they do for "feelers," whose emotions play a bigger role in communication and decision making. A thinker is often described as practical, a feeler as a people person. The terms aren't meant to be mutually exclusive; we have the capacity to operate in both styles. When thinkers and feelers pair up, they often depend on each other for balance. This can work if they value each other's primary mode. Differences become problems when they are seen as competitive rather than complementary. We usually stay rooted in our primary mode but can learn to operate in both modes.

A good ground rule for exploring intimacy is to understand that feelings are "real," meaning they describe what's really going on inside of us. They are our personal interpretations of the events or situations in our life; they're *right*, but they aren't necessarily *factual*. That is, what we feel might not match someone else's reality—our partner's, for example. A feeling, even a very strong one, that our partner is doing something "to" us may not be what's actually happening. On the other hand, it could be. Intimate communication relies on each of us clarifying our own thoughts and beliefs, and carefully listening to the other's without feeling threatened. We ask questions when we're unsure of our partner's meaning rather than making assumptions.

For example, the following phrases are helpful:

- "I'm hearing you say *[repeat what you heard]*. Is that what you're saying?"
- "I'm not sure I understand what you're saying. Can you say it another way?"

"Assumicide"

Perhaps the greatest barrier to intimacy is *assumicide* (another word that can't be found in the dictionary). It's the belief that there is one right way and assuming you have it. Things are seldom (possibly never) all one way or the other, and there's no place for absolutism in an intimate relationship. Emotions change; that's their nature. Sharing them makes us feel vulnerable; that's our nature. We need to feel safe to do it. Safety includes knowing your partner will respect your feelings, that your partner won't tease, ridicule, discount, or otherwise abuse them. We simply won't reveal our deep selves to someone who is critical, judgmental, or "knows it all."

When Two and Two Is Three

Even when undergoing the same events together, any two people are *always* having different experiences. Your interpretation of the situation—what it means emotionally for you—is your part of the story.

Intimacy doesn't require partners being on the same page. It's common to have different opinions and feelings as well as wants, needs, and skills. And none of that means we're in the wrong relationship with the wrong partner. As partners learn to share their stories respectfully and with curiosity—listening with the desire to learn from each other—something wonderful can happen. *An entirely new understanding can emerge that includes the best of both points of view.*

Intimacy can't be forced or demanded. It is a gift freely given, the result of love and trust. Intimacy grows even when you aren't watching it—it needs time and space. Healthy relationships require autonomy as well as togetherness. Couples need to develop a sense of togetherness and also breathing space for each to do his or her own thing.

EXERCISES

A Heartfelt Communication in Three Steps

Here is an easy three-step process that greatly improves the quality of intimate conversations. It sharpens our ability to step aside and listen to what a partner is saying from the heart. The process may seem stiff at first, but with practice it feels more natural.

1. Mirroring

Mirroring is repeating back the words and feelings that a partner is expressing. Take into account words, tone of voice, and body posture, as they all convey meaning. In repeating back, we can paraphrase the words, checking with our partner to make sure we are getting the essential message. (Remember, that's *mirroring*, not mocking.) Ask if you have it right and make adjustments until you do. You are not judging or evaluating, just mirroring back, letting your partner know his or her emotions are being successfully communicated. This alone often lowers the charge, but the process doesn't stop there. This exercise isn't just about calming the waters or damming them; it's about helping a partner get to the underlying issues and about finding a resolution.

2. Empathizing

Empathizing is letting your partner know that you recognize the emotional state and understand it. Remember, it doesn't matter if you agree or disagree with the feeling; you are connecting with your partner's emotion and validating it. An empathetic response is "I can see that you're really hurt. I'd be hurt, too." Or "I can see you are really mad. I've felt that way, too." Here are a couple of examples of what empathy is *not*: "I don't see why you feel that way." "What's the matter with you?"

3. Compassionate Action

Compassion means being moved by your partner's experience and wanting to help if possible. You do this by *asking* your partner what he or she needs. For example, "What do you need right now?" "How can I help you?" You stay true to your own needs, determining how you can accommodate both your partner's needs and yours. This is easily negotiated from a compassionate heart. For example, "I can't say

I'll never be late again, but I can promise I'll do my best to be on time, and I'll definitely call if there's a problem."

The Wonder of Silence

Intimacy happens by sharing feelings and also in the silence between encounters. This deeper, quieter level of being together is enhanced through prayer and meditation. When partners develop a spiritual practice together, they improve their chances of staying clean and sober and find greater levels of satisfaction with each other and with their relationship. This translates to the bedroom as well. In his book *Sex: The Catholic Experience,* Catholic priest and sociologist Andrew Greeley notes that couples who share lively spiritual lives together have better sex lives than those who don't.

When couples meditate together, they experience each other's sacredness; spiritual bonding is the strongest glue. Check the resources in the back of the book for more ideas.

Feelings Checklist

Intimate conversation becomes richer as your emotional vocabulary improves. You can learn words that express a great variety of moods beyond "okay" and "not so good." Review the list of feelings in appendix A of this book together and choose a few emotions that you'd like to have reflected in your relationship. Post them on the refrigerator, bathroom mirror, dashboard, and other places where you'll see them often. Talk about them, noticing when and where you experience them. Remember to always talk about what you want, not what you don't want. Tiger Woods sinks the putt by seeing it fall into the cup—not rimming the edge.

* * *

Intimacy is about being aware of our inner life and sharing it with our partner—it's a basic human need. We feel vulnerable when we share intimate thoughts and feelings, but as they are met with acceptance we feel loved. We can build our skills to improve intimacy and develop emotional awareness: they make interactions more satisfying.

But intimacy and partnering aren't one-size-fits-all deals. In the next chapter you'll read about three very different ways of forming partnership that honor different personal styles and meet different needs.

Chapter Four *

Three Relationship Styles:
Different Isn't Dysfunctional

Relationships come in various styles. Not only do we each have our own unique understanding of what a relationship should be, but we also have our own way of expressing ourselves in a relationship. Style determines how decisions are made, how conflict is resolved, and how communication and intimacy needs are met. Each of us has a personal style of relating.

We'll look at three common arrangements, described here as *merged/conforming, confronting/passionate,* and *avoiding/allowing.* All three are healthy and functional if built around love and respect. The three we've chosen aren't meant to be definitive, only to show that healthy differences exist. The examples show couples with matching modes to better illustrate how the styles work. These styles describe how people operate generally, not in every instance, and many of us won't neatly fit into any one category.

You can probably imagine all the various combinations and the trouble we can get into when we're in different modes and don't realize that these differences exist. This can be particularly true when addiction has dominated the

relationship. When partners, "having had a spiritual awakening," are suddenly looking at each other with eyes wide
open, they can be surprised, even shocked to discover they
don't have as much in common as they once thought.
Ideally a couple discovers their relationship style before committing, which reduces the potential for incompatible partnerships. It might not be likely for a confronting style
person and an avoiding one, for example, to make it to the
altar, but as you'll read in Lu and Phil's story, it happens.

The old saying "opposites attract" may encourage
people to believe that different styles will help to make the
relationship work, but successful partnering requires finding ways of working together. A Twelve Step recovery puts
us on a spiritual path, and as we have learned, challenges
are opportunities. We have a chance at reaching our ideal
love—one in which we are respectful and supportive of
each other and respectful of the needs of the relationship itself, regardless of our styles.

Remember: different doesn't have to mean dysfunctional.

The Merged/Conforming Relationship

The merged/conforming style has been the long-standing
custom. It is perhaps the way your grandparents' and possibly your parents' marriage functioned. According to most
experts, it's probably still the most common style. In a conforming marriage, one partner (usually the male) is dominant. Partners tend to follow traditional gender roles, with
the wife most likely taking care of children, home, and
health, and the husband taking care of business.

Television programs from past decades such as *Father
Knows Best* and *Leave It to Beaver* exemplify this style of marriage and family life. These popular shows represented

archetypes for at least two generations who grew up with them as prime-time viewing, then as afternoon reruns. We might still hear references to the Cleavers as the "ideal" family.

In a merged/conforming style, problems are resolved by listening politely. Partners take turns presenting their case. Attempts at convincing the other to come around to his or her point of view are respectful. Heated debate and rigorous argument are rare. If a point isn't easily won, or agreement not readily accomplished, conforming couples find a compromise both can live with. When it comes to the final decision, the dominant partner generally casts the deciding vote. Conforming couples tend to get along well, and family life is smooth. Personal identity and self-interest are expressed through the relationship—meaning what is good for the marriage and family is good for the individual. Communication and intimacy between partners are limited and generally at the discretion of the dominant partner. Again, this isn't necessarily a problem when both partners agree that it works best for them. In its ideal form it is a stable, time-honored arrangement.

Challenges to This Relationship Style
Cultural patterns have changed, and for the most part this traditional marriage formula hasn't kept up with the times. Today many women are better educated than their mothers and grandmothers, and are used to making decisions. They have the opportunity to be financially independent; many contribute substantially to the family finances. At the same time, men are rethinking their role as the sole breadwinner and the effects of this arrangement on their health and happiness.

Potential problems with a conventional marriage are that the relationship takes precedence over individuality, and self-development can suffer at the expense of maintaining order—which is the overriding value. This can lead to anger and resentment if either partner feels stifled by the arrangement. In a conforming arrangement, one partner expresses more power than the other, and inequality always has the potential for abuse. The health of this system relies heavily on the sensitivity of the dominant partner. Factors to be looked at are the need for accountability, how differences are handled, and whether both voices are heard and respected.

THE CONFRONTING/PASSIONATE RELATIONSHIP

Here, *confronting/passionate* describes how partners approach problem solving; it does not necessarily describe their personality types. But these people do tend to be volatile risk-takers. They thrive on differences of opinion and don't shy away from sharing them. It is described as *confronting/passionate* as both communication and intimacy are hot and spicy. Partners enjoy their high level of engagement, competition, and heated discussions. The relationship doesn't suffer by this ongoing struggle—in fact it is fed by it.

Couples in a healthy confronting/passionate relationship style fill the intervals between arguments with good times together, laughter, affection, and passionate sex. Individuality is a high value here, and power is equally expressed. In contrast to the careful listening of the conforming folks, confronting/passionate couples tend to interrupt, override, and even try to out-shout each other. The road to resolution is often rocky, but their arguments are eventually settled; often whoever puts up the best fight wins until the next skirmish begins. Provided that partners maintain love and respect and reach a healthy balance between the volatile bouts and quieter times, this is a viable arrangement.

In the television series *Roseanne*, popular in the 1980s and 1990s, Dan and Roseanne Conner's marriage portrayed this style. It was riddled with conflict and passion, and at the same time, the two characters were clearly on the same side. When they joined forces they fiercely defended their home and offspring against harm.

Challenges to This Style

Ideally, confronting couples fight fair, their arguments are principled, and points are respectfully won. However, such sparring risks becoming destructive, creating hurt feelings and lasting damage. Honesty (at all costs) is usually a positive value, but "taking each other's inventory" under the guise of truthfulness pushes the boundaries of good judgment, particularly in the heat of battle when the gloves come off. If an argument crosses the line into insults, sarcasm, or other destructive behaviors, it would no longer qualify as confronting; it would be unhealthy.

The success of this style depends on the authenticity of the partners. It avoids destruction when it is a genuine expression of spirit, and remains healthy and vibrant as long as it isn't mean-spirited or demeaning. Partners need to confine their confronting to principles, not personalities. There will most likely be areas of sensitivity for one or the other partner, and personal boundaries must be respected.

The Avoiding/Allowing Relationship

Avoiding/allowing couples de-emphasize conflict and make light of disagreements. Whereas confronting couples are looking for a good scrap, avoiding couples go around the block to avoid one. In many ways, these two styles are the mirror opposites of each other. When avoiding couples air differences, which they do occasionally, they listen to each other respectfully, but nothing really changes. They don't resolve differences like the first two styles. They don't attempt to persuade, compromise, or duke it out; they often come to terms by agreeing to disagree. Theirs is a "live and let live" philosophy, and they focus on what they have in common. They place a high value on their partnership but an even higher one on letting each other be who they are.

These partners tend to form their own friendships and attend to separate activities. It is a life lived by principles, and the level of engagement and intimacy is low. Couples care deeply for one another and form deep and lasting bonds—but the binding force is on values and commitment to projects or way of life. An example of an avoiding/ allowing relationship might be found in marriages where profession takes precedence over spouse and family.

Challenges to This Style

The film *The Preacher's Wife* portrays the potential pitfalls of this kind of marriage, as well as the satisfaction of a life lived in service to principles. Challenges to an avoiding partnership lie in maintaining separate lives with enough togetherness to sustain a relationship. Partners may have different needs at different times, and it's not clear how well these needs can be sensitively accommodated. The low level of communication poses additional challenges to child rearing. Avoiding couples often lack interpersonal skills to solve problems, and in the face of life's big challenges, the relationship may fall apart. This style walks a thin line between "live and let live" and denial. While it offers stability, satisfaction, and longevity, it can also create loneliness. Couples may miss the opportunity to discover deeper parts of themselves and each other.

The Recovering Relationship

The relationship style we naturally gravitate to and find most comfortable often genuinely reflects who we are. It won't change a lot, and it doesn't necessarily need to, if we can work together and find middle ground. Small compromises can make the difference. Success comes through personal awareness, the commitment to grow together, and the willingness to develop new skills. All relationships are a practice in acceptance and patience; they are opportunities for continued self-development. Couples who are having difficulty in their partnerships due to genuine differences in style can take heart from recovery principles. Diversity in beliefs and style are found throughout the recovering community. Differences are resolved by group conscience guided by principles and a sense of higher purpose. Granted, this happens in hourly segments, but it is teaching us that it can be done and showing us how.

Lu and Phillip's Story

Lu identifies her style as *confronting* but acknowledges that in recovery she has lost some of her desire to stay up all night and argue. Lu lives with Phillip, a skilled *avoider*. These opposite approaches are a problem for them. Lu doesn't feel heard, and Phillip feels criticized by her complaints and takes her expressions of frustration about the relationship personally. They're on the brink of calling the relationship off—although they love each other and in many important ways are a good match.

Phil is aware of Lu's dissatisfaction and is sympathetic. But he holds to the philosophy of noninterference and believes that problems solve themselves when left alone. He is right to some extent, but Lu's frustration is not going away, either. There is an edge in her voice, and it is getting sharper. Phillip is tired of her growing anger but has made it clear by his disengagement that he isn't going to "work it out" with her. He doesn't want to end their relationship. He loves Lu and feels things will settle down with time. This is beyond Lu's comprehension at this point, but she has decided to give the avoiding method a try. "What's to lose?" she asked, and quickly answered her own question. "Only six months."

Lu committed to practicing an avoiding style for six months, doing it one day at a time. She used spiritual principles—"turning it over"—and prayed and meditated often. Altars popped up all over the house like dandelions in May. She talked regularly with her sponsor and attended more meetings to deal with her irritation. Three months into it she said she was getting the hang of it. She kept notes on issues she felt were really important, planning to take them up with Phil at the end of the experiment. To her surprise, she said her list was getting shorter rather than longer. "Some of the things were actually disappearing," she said in amazement.

By the end of the allotted time, Lu felt far more in control of herself and more serene than before. She had eliminated almost everything on her list. Her experience taught her the difference in her own mind between needing to talk and wanting to talk. However, she insisted that Phil commit to engage with her when she really needed him to. The idea of never working things out together didn't feel like recovery to her. It felt like denial.

Phil agreed to pay attention to Lu when she needs him to—although *paying attention* hadn't been the problem; *confronting the issues and resolving them* had. Phil agreed to learn a conflict management technique with Lu—and then practice it. That's as far as their story goes at this time. Lu feels she has grown spiritually and her gratitude-to-frustration ratio has greatly improved—which she feels is a miracle in itself. If Phil is going to adjust his avoiding style toward the middle, he is far more apt to do it in the climate of affirmation Lu is creating. But he will have to see it as a value in order to make the change.

Partnerships aren't a fifty-fifty arrangement; they require 100 percent from each person. In this moment, Lu is way ahead on the score sheet—but keeping score is seldom a good idea. In dealing with their situation, Lu took what was the high road for her, using the challenge as an opportunity for self-improvement. Phil made the concession he could make and agreed to learn a new skill.

Recovering relationships, like the people in them, are in the process of growing and changing. Lu and Phil are committed to each other for the long haul, and the long haul happens one day at a time. To paraphrase the discussion in the Big Book, the promises are fulfilled sometimes quickly, sometimes slowly, but will always materialize if we work for them.

Abuse Isn't a Style

The relationship styles and the challenges we've looked at represent healthy differences that can be worked through using program wisdom and counseling, when needed. Partners cross a line when they act out angry feelings or any other abusive behaviors, and this can happen in any relationship style. Abuse is broadly defined as behavior that makes another person uncomfortable and continues even when we are told to stop. Abuse isn't a style; it's a serious disorder. Environments that predict abuse include active addiction, power inequities, and secrecy. Abuse can be obvious, such as in matters of personal safety. But there may be more subtle indicators, too. Use these questions to help reveal them.

- How comfortable am I with the information mentioned above?
- Do I feel like I have to keep my feelings about these issues a secret from my partner and others?
- How much explaining do I have to do to my mate?
- Is name calling, ridicule, or physical abuse going on?
- Are there threats of any kind?
- Is there a pattern of emotional neglect or withdrawal of affection?
- Am I comfortable with how sex is expressed?
- Am I concerned about any aspect of my partner's sexual behavior toward others, including children?
- Am I concerned about my partner's use of Internet sex or pornographic material of any kind?

There are community resources for handling domestic abuse. If you can't find what you need, make a phone call (anonymously if need be) to a counselor, minister, or sponsor.

Cultivating a Spirit of Cooperation

When trying to work through relationship styles, merely *not fighting* isn't good enough; we need to actively court the spirit of cooperation. Cooperation involves intentionally working together for the good of the partnership—but not sacrificing ourself to it or *working it all the time*. The spirit of cooperation is one of fair play: it can't rely on one person always giving in and one always making decisions. Weighing, measuring, and recording every interaction won't accomplish the principle of fairness, either. It's called the *spirit of cooperation* because it isn't easily quantified, but you know when you have it and you miss it when you don't.

Exercises

Points of Agreement

If you and your partner have different relationship styles, locate areas of agreement. Remember you are talking style, not substance: for example, the way decisions are made, not the decisions themselves. Most style differences can be resolved when both agree to work together with the spirit of cooperation.

Principles Before Personalities

The Twelve Step principles are what hold the meeting structure together and allow differences to be expressed at meetings without argument. Read the Twelve Traditions in the Big Book or *Twelve Steps and Twelve Traditions*. Take one principle at a time and talk about how to make it part of your relationship.

* * *

This chapter looked at three styles of relationships and saw that different doesn't mean dysfunctional. Certain behaviors and attitudes can improve your chances of having a good relationship regardless of your style. Cultivating a spirit of cooperation and living by principles can guide you toward your unique vision. Next you'll read about levels of awareness: how you can slip out of the moment and how to step back into it.

Chapter Five *

Favorite Fights and Fighting Fair

Regardless of relationship style, most couples seem to argue about the same things. The five basic arguments are about money, sex, time, children, and extended family. They are really like five branches on the same tree—a cluster of inter-related attitudes and behaviors rooted in a lack of self-esteem and the power struggle that we wage in the hope of filling up an empty space inside us. Our arguments may function as our addiction once did, as distractions from our discomfort and as futile attempts to feel powerful.

As we rely more on our Higher Power for our security, we argue less.

THE MONEY FIGHT

Money has come to represent many things in our culture: power, security, time, personal success, even love. With all that freight, it's no wonder we can become so confused about finances. Money is one of the most common areas of disagreement in partnerships and the one most often cited for breakups.

Marriages are businesses. Even when the arrangement doesn't include marriage, a couple's money will mingle. It can be an issue as soon as the first date! Debtors Anonymous (DA) literature discusses terminal vagueness—not knowing exactly how much money we have or where it goes. Good partnerships, like good businesses, are based on clear agreements. Even couples who are otherwise spiritually fit will benefit from discussing and agreeing on how they will handle finances, because there's no mistaking it. Each of us comes to the table with our own set of deep-seated beliefs around money and understanding those beliefs, let alone changing them, takes some work.

Living beyond our means and being miserly are flip sides of the same coin. They're about fear and poor self-esteem, and they result in dishonesty. Getting clear on finances brings freedom and self-appreciation, and it restores honesty. We get to decide how much is enough and how to spend it. But when we are living a lie, we run the risk of losing our sobriety. If money and debt are causing problems in our relationship, there is help. We can attend DA meetings, read literature on getting out of debt, and seek professional financial counseling.

Build Your Money Management Skills

Here are a few ideas on money management to get you and your partner started on a clear-headed discussion. Suggestion: when you and your partner are ready to start, take a few moments to center and begin your discussion by asking your Higher Power's guidance and support.

Take a Financial Inventory

- Make an accurate record of monthly household income figures—write them down.

- Make an accurate record of monthly expenses and bills, including estimated taxes and debts—write them down.
- Be clear about credit card debts—write them down.
- Discuss debt in general. When debt is brought into the partnership there will be questions about whether it should be divided and if so, how. Talk about it.
- Discuss what funds you hold individually and jointly. Is your current arrangement working well? Keep in mind that once you are clear about who pays for what, separate accounts work well for most of us; we need autonomy.

Create a Monthly Spending Plan

DA uses the positive term "spending plan," as "budget" sounds restrictive to most people.

- Work on the plan together to avoid misunderstandings. Think about fixed expenses, variable expenses, seasonal expenses, savings. Many good books on money management are available.
- If you haven't already banked a "prudent reserve"— three to six months' worth of expenses—start building one now and include contributions in your monthly plan.
- Create a household bill-paying system. Keep an "office." This can be as simple as a shoebox, but make it a place to keep unpaid bills, checkbook, stamps, envelopes, and a file for paid bills. Agree on a time to review bills and tend to business. Decide who pays which and when: who writes and mails the check, who makes an online payment, and so on.

• Decide on a regular time to review your monthly
  plan, maybe weekly at first, monthly or even quar-
  terly after you both have the hang of it. (Don't wait
  until April 14!) Use the time to discuss how your
  plan is working—and how you both feel about it.
  Renegotiate if you need to.

Discuss Discretionary and Spontaneous Purchases

• We all need discretionary funds—a few dollars to
  call our own. Feelings of deprivation can lead to
  overspending, as DA literature tells us. We need to
  find the point where we aren't feeling deprived, yet
  are meeting basic needs, building that prudent reserve, and having some money to spend on little
  luxuries. Agree on a fair figure and know that the
  agreement can be renegotiated. We don't have to
  be accountable for discretionary money.
• In addition, many couples have a policy to allow
  for spur-of-the-moment household purchases out
  of shared funds—those "blue-light specials" that
  are just too good to pass up. Agree on how much
  either of you can spend without consulting with
  the other, then stick with the agreement.

Know the Basics

• Make sure you both know the basics about money:
  balancing the checkbook, how interest works,
  credit cards, loans, how to read your bills.
• Carefully investigate the rules around your credit
  cards and your use of them. Financial advisors recommend paying cards off each month or getting
  rid of them; DA literature advises cutting up credit
  cards. If you are using them as a loan source, know
  the interest rate and how it works—read the small
  print. Credit card companies can change your inter-

est rate without notifying you. If either of you is a compulsive gambler or compulsive spender, use cash only.

Keep It Simple

- Having less doesn't have to mean forced frugality. It's about living with the mind-set that the less you own, the easier (and better) life gets. Start to get a feel for "less is more" by getting rid of clutter, room by room. When you eliminate what you don't need or no longer want, you open up doors for what you really do need. You reduce any sense of wastefulness, and you feel better about yourself, your surroundings, and the environment.
- Many books are available about living on less—but keep in mind that you can cross the line into stinginess. Pick some cost-reducing practices that feel comfortable to you. You don't have to cut back on everything, everywhere. Here's a short list of cost-cutting activities to get you thinking: Turn off lights when you're not in the room, regulate the thermostat, consolidate trips to the store, use a grocery list, eat at home more often, avoid expensive coffee shops, know the limits on your cell phone minutes and how much you pay for roaming and overage.

Money Issues: More Than Meets the Eye

When a financial issue comes up, notice if it's a money problem, a personal problem, or a relationship problem. Then address it from the right perspective. For example, if you're leaving the lights on because you still resent your parents telling you to turn them off, you might want to let it go now that you're paying the bill. Consider a Fourth Step on money and spending. Identify the emotional factors that you address through spending—including being a pinchpenny. If you have the money but go without necessities, the Fourth Step can bring some needed clarity. Additional considerations: Are you shopping compulsively? How would you define compulsive shopping? Are addictions such as gambling draining family resources? How would you identify a problem in this area?

FIGHTING FOR TIME

Time slips through our fingers in much the same way money does when we're not paying attention. Taking control of our time is about making it work for us, not against us. It gives us the chance to find enough time to do the things we want to do—including "wasting" it, if that's what we prefer.

We may divide our time differently, but we're all working with twenty-four hours each day. Arguments about time are often over how we spend it; specifically, is there enough for you and me and the relationship? Too much time apart can be detrimental to the relationship; not enough time for self can jeopardize personal growth and recovery.

The following list of questions can help shed light on whether you or a partner need to balance the time sheet. You can take it separately or as a "we" test. Rate these questions on a scale of one (strong yes) to five (strong no). There's no score sheet. Use your answers for self-reflection and possibly a conversation.

Are we / Am I . . .
_____ going to bed too tired?
_____ waking up angry?
_____ carrying too much debt?
_____ maintaining good health practices, including exercise?
_____ spending time with friends?

____ spending enough time puttering or just
hanging out?
____ working too much?
____ getting enough down time?
____ finding time to be together?
____ attending enough meetings?
____ singing in the shower often enough?
____ laughing and playing enough? *(including spur-
of-the-moment activities such as a picnic or making
love in the afternoon)*

Ask yourselves: What would I do if time and money were
not an issue, and I knew they wouldn't become an issue?
Talk about it together.

Stretching Time

Stress is a side effect of living with a time crunch. It doesn't
always surface as a specific argument, but it creates a dis-
agreeable climate where arguments flourish. It is also an at-
mosphere where relapse is more likely. Consider making a
detailed schedule of how you spend each moment of your
week—including all activities, travel time, meetings, time
spent talking with friends—and see exactly where it goes.
You don't have to do this forever, but it will help you get
real about your time commitments. Getting real helps break
the habit of over-scheduling. Showing up on time breaks
the habit of keeping others waiting. It gives us more enjoy-
able time.

ARGUMENTS ABOUT SEX

It is probably no surprise that sex has made it into the top
five arguments list. While it may be the one we are most
invested in, arguing about sex probably yields the least

satisfaction. Think about it—do you want to have sex with a partner who is pressuring you? Do you want to have sex with a partner who is telling you no? Most counselors say the biggest argument of all is the sex/housework dilemma. Most men want more sex, and because women are still considered to be in charge of the home, they want more help with housework. That seems like a good place to begin problem solving. For more on this topic you can turn to chapter 8, "Gender: Friend or Foe?" and chapter 9: "Sex, Spirituality, and Satisfaction." Resolving our differences about sex makes sense, and it results in more sex more often with a lot more satisfaction.

Fighting Over Children

While our sex argument may be the least productive, a fight about the children may be the most destructive. Yet we do it. Many of us became parents before we had finished growing up. Others who may have had well-planned families didn't plan on addiction and the toll it takes on the family. It's fair to say none of us want to hurt the kids.

Addiction is a generational disease, and many of us struggle to raise our families in recovery without falling back into the same patterns we were raised with. Without a conscious intervention, we are likely to either repeat the past or overcompensate to avoid repeating it. Parenting classes are a way of learning new skills and are offered at little or no cost in most communities. Check with your local church or social agency. You can always find books on child rearing at the library. Consider finding a mentor or a sponsor. This goes for recovering families who have children as well as couples who are considering becoming parents.

With today's blended families, children may be getting

different instructions from different sets of parents. We can fight over whose weekend it is to be where; the dress code; what's acceptable in music, friends, and food; how to be supportive; how to discipline; and almost everything else. Good communication among all the players is important. But even then parents have different child rearing philosophies, and often we don't know how different until we're in the middle of a disagreement. Chapter 10, "Help for the Nonaddicted Partner," discusses using principles as a way of raising our kids. It's a highly interactive process that helps kids develop the tools they need to make decisions.

As for incentive in resolving the argument over kids, remember, this isn't about us, it's about them. Recovery gives us a second chance in many cases, and that's about grace.

The Extended Family Fight

Families are funny animals. They're the best and the worst of us. We hear people in recovery say that when they got sober, relations with the whole family seemed to get better, too. But just as many talk about getting clean, getting a program, and having to realize that the folks at home haven't changed.

Extended family is all relatives other than our mate and children. Fights about extended family are often rooted in boundaries and loyalties. Where do we draw the lines, and what are our responsibilities? We all have our own answers. A rule of thumb is that while we won't regret the past nor wish to shut the door on it, as the promises say, we don't have to leave it standing wide open, either. Finding the balance point between extended family life and immediate family life and all that is required in maintaining our own lives is not simple. Consider the following scenarios.

His aunt talks too much, and his uncle drinks too much. Yet if they're not invited to the birthday celebration, your mother-in-law will lay a guilt trip the size of Montana on your partner—and that means six more sessions of therapy. You point this out to your guy, but it ends up in a big fight as always.

Your brother laughs too loud and teases the dog. Your sister uses drugs and is on probation and wants to borrow more money. Your husband doesn't hide the fact that he doesn't like your family, and you're hiding the fact that you've slipped your sister a fifty. You're both angry, and after everyone leaves you get into it *again*. He accuses you of going behind his back, and you lie, even as you wonder how you'll come up with an extra fifty.

His father rants about the evils of gay marriage, and your brother is gay. You'd like to say something, but your husband has that *don't cross my father* look on his face. You stifle it for now but get into a fight on the way home.

Why won't he stand up for you? His cousin has been sleeping on your couch for six weeks while he's looking for work. He borrows your car, brings it home with an empty tank, and isn't paying for groceries. Your husband has a blind spot about the whole thing. They were like brothers growing up in an alcoholic home.

If extended family is a source of too many arguments, consider drawing lines—but draw them together. And realize that they'll have to be erased and redrawn on occasions. Holidays, special birthdays, weddings, the birth of a child, and the needs of aging parents are some of the inevitable occasions when the heart overrules logic, and we show up with a gift and the right outfit regardless of the emotional price tag. We can talk about it later at a meeting!

We can set boundaries around our time, limit our interactions with members we don't get along with, and lobby to hold family gatherings at a neutral place such as a restaurant rather than at home. A family reunion can be held at a state park where there's lots of room to visit and to take a walk when you need to. We can pray for guidance and treat the entire encounter with family as fertile ground for a Twelfth Step, paying special attention to attraction, not promotion.

Mates need to make it clear to each other that they come first. This alone creates a new order. It makes it clear that you're on the same side and takes a lot of heat out of the battles. We have the right to not show up at family events or to let our partner off the hook if it means running the risk of relapse. The bottom line is that our first responsibility is to our *immediate* family—mates and kids. Everyone else is outside that circle. If any relative has been abusive or the potential is there, it's our job to keep the kids safe as well as ourselves. We can't fix our extended families, but we can love them. Sometimes distance does indeed make the heart grow fonder.

EXERCISES

Fighting Fair: Some Rules of Engagement
Knowing about the top five arguments doesn't mean you won't get into them, but it might provide perspective. Arguing can be healthy when you observe a few rules. Suggestion: take a few moments to center and begin your discussion by asking your Higher Power's guidance and support.

1. Avoid approaching each other when your tempers are high (progress, not perfection).
2. Make an appointment to talk when both of you are cooled down and have had time to gather your

thoughts (see "Pause When Agitated" below). Set time limits for your talk.

3. Don't vent or get out your list of grievances; focus on one topic per session.

4. Direct remarks at a behavior without labeling your partner. No name-calling or angry outbursts. If this happens, you need to take responsibility for your behavior.

5. Table your discussion when the time is up, using a closing ritual as suggested below.

Pause When Agitated

In discussing Step Eleven, the Big Book reminds us to *pause when agitated or doubtful and ask for the right thought or action.* In following this advice, it can be difficult to stop the train— the thought train, that is. While prayer is when we talk to God, meditation is when we listen. Learning a few easy-to-do meditations will increase impulse control and greatly reduce the tendency to fly off the handle at a mate.

We don't have to sit on a purple cushion and chant. Meditation, in its simplest form, is relaxation. Activities such as gardening, puttering, hiking, sitting by a stream and watching the water flow are meditative. They calm the thinking mind and allow a new thought to enter your system. Most meditation uses breath to calm and center. In that quiet space we can get free of our habitual thinking patterns. Translated into recovery talk, this means it gets our inner squirrel off the wheel and makes it less likely we'll do the same old thing we've done before while expecting different results.

The following exercise begins with breathing to slow us down and draw our spirits inward. Taking three deep breaths helps; taking three more helps more.

"Pause When Agitated" Meditation

Right now, notice your breath. How deeply into your body are you breathing? Are you holding your breath? Slowly draw in a breath. Hold it for a few seconds and let it out—slowly and fully. Take six more deep breaths slowly, one at a time. As you take these deep breaths, pay attention to how the air feels as it is going in your nostrils. Feel it going down the back of your throat. Notice how it feels as your belly expands. Take in as much breath as possible, extending your belly. As you exhale, feel your muscles letting go. Notice how your shoulders let go. Notice how your back lets go. Notice how your stomach lets go. Open your eyes and notice how you feel. You have just meditated. You can close your eyes and repeat this process again—right now.

Further practice allows you to relax deeper and longer. There isn't anything you have to do, no great thoughts, nothing. It is the opposite of doing anything. That is the point. Do nothing and experiencing being.

Make it a practice to pause and breathe until you feel calm before approaching your partner when you are agitated.

Negotiating Solutions

The following exercise provides a way of exploring differences and finding creative solutions. Practice it before you actually need it, and wait until tempers cool down before you actually use it.

Suggestion: first take a few moments to center and begin your discussion by asking your Higher Power's guidance and support.

1. Identify the problem together—when you agree on the crux of the conflict, write it on the top of two pieces of notebook size paper, one for each of you.

2. Now list the feelings this conflict is bringing up for you. If you are still experiencing the feelings, wait until you can talk about them but not experience them.

3. Identify acceptable solutions for you and write them down on your paper. You might begin with some pretty far-out solutions. Don't edit; just write. Allowing yourself to be as absurd as you want allows the rebel part of you to let off a little steam. Write until you are finished.

4. Eventually you will choose three to six possible solutions that you feel are the most authentic. Write them on a new piece of paper and exchange these solutions with your partner. As a couple, pick one you both find acceptable. If there isn't one, choose one that comes close, then negotiate back and forth until you can agree. Make sure the solution will work for both of you and that you will agree to give it a go.

5. Have a closing ritual such as exchanging a hug. It will let you know if the solution feels right. If there is a hesitation when you close, you may have to table the discussion for now and come back to it later.

* * *

Differences are a natural part of relationships. They aren't necessarily problems if we are open to resolving them. That means finding creative solutions. Arguments indicate that we're attached to an old way. Fighting tenaciously indicates we are trying to get our way. Solutions are about finding a new way.

Next we'll read more about the ongoing process of self-awareness and how to be more present in the relationship.

Chapter Six *

The Journey to Awareness

Kinetta hears the edge in her voice and wonders why she is crabby at Marc so much of the time. Marc feels pathetic hiding behind the newspaper making faces at her. Both wonder if they made a huge mistake. Getting married seemed like the right thing at the time, but about three months into their marriage they started coming undone. Kinetta has begun to sound more like her mother than herself, and Marc is acting like a four-year-old too much of the time. Neither likes what's going on inside themselves or in their marriage. These troubling interactions leave them unsatisfied and more than a bit mystified.

We learned in previous chapters that the desire to have a relationship is instinctive, but how we go about it is learned behavior. Kinetta and Marc absorbed some unhealthy ideas about love and marriage growing up. Family patterns keep us locked in childhood strategies until we realize what we're doing and make efforts to change. Now, without knowing it, their early patterns have surfaced and are threatening their relationship. As we know from other areas

of recovery, the pain and disappointment of self-defeating
behavior can be a rude but effective alarm clock.

Like Kinetta and Marc, we can be surprised to find ourselves acting like the parents we vowed never to be like—or
reacting like the kid we thought we'd left behind. It's easy to
think our partner is causing it—doing it to us. We can even
find evidence to support our "case." Recovery promises
that more shall be revealed, and in most cases the revelation
comes from within. As fellow seeker Thomas Merton reminds us, the first step toward finding God is to discover
the truth about ourselves. Recovery has taught us that facing those inner demons calls for both humility and humor.
It's the journey to awareness.

Who's Driving the Bus?

The 1970s saw the popularization of a helpful model for
understanding the human psyche: Transactional Analysis.
In the classic book *I'm OK—You're OK*, author Thomas A.
Harris, M.D. describes three primary states of mind, or ego
states: child, parent, and adult. Each state of mind has particular thoughts, emotions, abilities, attitudes, and behaviors that correspond to the age and stage of development
they represent. All three states are important to being a
well-balanced person, and the goal is to be able to count on
them to do their jobs *appropriately,* meaning acting in
the right persona at the right time, and this calls for self-
awareness and usually a little healing.

These three ego states stay with us for life. The child within
us doesn't grow up but remains a child. It gives us flexibil-
ity, curiosity, willingness to forgive, and perhaps most important, hope. On the other hand, if we were wounded in

childhood and haven't healed, the pain continues into adult years—often as fear, depression, or anxiety. In recovery, as we heal we start feeling happy, joyous, and free more often. The healthy parent ego relates to our ability to nurture ourselves and stay on track with self-care throughout life. A toxic inner parent might also show up as neglect, guilt, and other self-abusive tendencies.

The healthy adult ego takes care of business and career decisions. It's our public face. An out-of-balance adult psyche can be out of touch with our personal needs, making us rigid, uncaring, or insensitive. In contrast, an underdeveloped adult psyche lacks the skills necessary for success in the world. The adult state is the part of us that is primarly involved in our relationship. Ironically, it's often the least developed aspect of self in the addicted psyche.

In addition to the parent, adult, and child, we're adding the terms "rebel" and "higher self" to more fully understand the inner workings of the recovering mind.

The rebel is included for obvious reasons: it is almost always the prevailing part in addiction. The rebel hates rules, balks at authority—shoots from the hip and asks questions later. In recovery the rebel stays with us, but its dangerous risk-taking tendencies give way to more positive adventurousness. The healed rebel keeps his edge, but isn't as likely to go over it.

The higher self represents our ideal recovering self. It is the voice of reason and good sense, and it indicates our connection to a Higher Power. This aspect reflects Twelve Step program principles.

All five aspects can be seen as coexisting parts of our personality or character. Let's take a closer look at each one and learn how they influence our relationships in both positive and negative ways.

Meet Your Parent

Ideally, our inner parent nurtures and protects our inner child, reminding us to eat our vegetables, tie our shoes, and go out and play. It becomes a problem in the relationship when we direct that energy toward our partner. We all need TLC now and again, but under most conditions, it's not appropriate to become the primary caretaker of another adult. When both partners are caught in their parent ego, the partnership suffers. It will be riddled with power struggles and self-righteousness thinly disguised in phrases such as "I'm only telling you this for your own good."

Our parent ego is often subconsciously looking for a child to take care of and can be attracted to an irresponsible person. Likewise, an irresponsible person can be subconsciously looking for a caretaker. Either way, it's not an equal match.

Alternatively, a healed internal parent makes us feel secure and well cared for. We naturally act more loving to our partner and others, too. The lists below show the difference: the column on the left shows what a toxic takeover might look like. The column on the right shows a recovery "makeover" of that tendency.

Toxic Parent Takeover	*Recovered Parent Makeover*
Neglects	Nurtures
Smothers	Supports
Shames (self or others)	Encourages
Manipulates	Communicates
Controls	Protects
Resents	Forgives

Reclaiming the Child

Our inner child contains our honest, open, and willing heart. It trusts and is affectionate and loving, but also needs protection. Without a well-developed parent in our psyche, the child is too vulnerable; it doesn't know whom to trust.

In a relationship, our child aspect needs to know the rules and needs them to be fair. We never outgrow our need for positive reinforcement—kind words and stars on the refrigerator. This holds true even in our adult relationships. Love is built on compliments, not criticism.

A neglected inner child results in unhealthy dependencies. A needy partner can overwhelm a relationship. And turning our life and will over to the care of another is a recipe for resentment. A reclaimed inner child is reflected in a lively imagination, creativity, playfulness, health, and well-being. Feelings of security and trust translate into being trustworthy ourselves. Consider the differences:

Wounded Child Takeover	*Healed Child Makeover*
Insecure	Spontaneous
Shut down	Imaginative
Fearful	Trusting
Feels guilty or shamed	Playful
Overwhelmed	Asks for help
Jaded	Innocent

The Rebel Yell
The rebel is spirited, but not mean-spirited. This aspect of self is often just out for a good time. Rebellion is part of being a teenager, and there's a time and place for healthy dissent. And there's a difference between thoughtful nonconformity and bucking the system for no good reason. The rebel is the part of us that fights injustice and is willing to take a stand even if it means standing alone. A healed rebel has a spirit of adventure rather than revolting simply for its own sake. Sensitivity to our rebellious nature requires an honest respect of freedom—not just railing against authority.

The rebel's independent spirit can be refreshingly liberated from other people's opinions and, combined with insight from other parts of our psyche, eventually become an asset.

But regarding a relationship: the rebel just isn't all that into it. Healthy relating depends on cooperation, and an overactive rebel is not the part of us that we can count on for mutuality in problem solving.

The rebel's skills are usually limited to a *love it or leave it* attitude. In the first chapter we noted that it was impossible to be in a committed relationship with one foot out the door—but that's the rebel's favorite stance. Issuing decrees or mandates doesn't go down well in anyone's relationship. In a recovering relationship, it's almost certainly going to trigger the rebel. Rebels often pair up with other rebels or authoritarian types, to assure them of a good fight. As recovery continues, impulse control gradually replaces our "quick on the draw" tendencies.

As we've seen, this book is filled with problem-solving techniques, suggestions for good communication, and skill-building exercises. The challenge is to keep the rebel busy in the other room while you practice them in your adult mind!

Addictive Rebel Takeover	*Recovered Rebel Makeover*
Willfully rebellious	Independent
Danger-seeking	Adventurous
Fights any authority	Questions authority
Hot-headed	Cool-headed
Out of control	Freedom-loving
Insecure	Courageous

The Adult: Reasonable and Sensitive

Think of the recovered adult self as someone you'd enjoy knowing—or being. The adult is both reasonable and sensitive, combining compassion with clear thinking and making decisions that are well considered and appropriate to the circumstances. The adult is objective but not dissociated. The adult controls impulses and expresses emotions appropriately. Our adult self pays attention to the reactions of others and respects feelings, but doesn't make decisions based purely on emotions—our own or others'. In the adult state of mind we are present, reacting to what's happening now. This part of us understands life and how to be successful, and provides a reality check—keeping us from being too naive or too skeptical. It carries the values of hope, strength, and experience.

A dysfunctional adult mind relies too heavily on logic to the exclusion of feelings. A steady diet of "pure" reason creates heartburn! Being overly critical crushes the spirit, shutting down creativity. An out-of-balance adult mind makes snap judgments and is inflexible. Once a proclamation has been issued there's no negotiating. On the other side of the coin, an underdeveloped adult self might tend to be wishy-washy, refuse to set boundaries, or fail to participate in the relationship.

Dysfunctional Adult Takeover	*Recovered Adult Makeover*
Makes snap judgments	Thinks out options
Overrules/Disconnects	Is sensitive, in touch
Is controlling	Is accepting
Is inflexible	Is reasonable
Is judgmental	Is thoughtful
Knows it all	Is curious

Higher Self/Lower Self

Our recovering self learns from life's experiences and gains wisdom. This self carries our highest values, reminding us to be of service, but at the same time, it has not lost touch with the human side. It combines the best of all the characters we've looked at. Our higher self has the love and concern of a good parent, the disarming innocence of the child, and a rebellious streak that keeps us from becoming sanctimonious. In addition to reflecting healthy adult behavior, our higher self might also serve as sort of an ideal grandparent—one with a seasoned, wise point of view. It understands life's dilemmas and is sensitive to the struggles we face. It sees things from our perspective as well as keeping an eye on the big picture.

But because everything contains its opposite, being in touch with our higher nature means accepting our lower nature. In recovery we accept that the potential of slipping back into old behavior is ever-present. Whether we are resolving a relationship conflict, handling office politics, talking with our children, or relaxing on the weekend, the choice is always there. Recovery lies in striving for awareness.

Lower Self Takeover	*Higher Self Makeover*
Foolhardy	Wise
Resentful	Forgiving
Self-serving	Serves others
Uncaring	Compassionate
Closed-minded	Open-minded
Addicted	Walks in "sunlight of the spirit"

How It Works

These five aspects of self can help us interpret our own feelings and behaviors. When a problem takes over, it has the potential to take up all our attention, making it seem much bigger than it is. We lose perspective. Becoming familiar with these five "profiles," knowing their possible flashpoints, provides containment. It's like tending a fire in only one room, not letting the entire house go up in flames. For example, when we feel overwhelmed in our marriage, it's a pretty good indication that our inner child has taken over. If we feel like slamming the door, hot-wiring the neighbor's motorcycle, and disappearing into a vapor trail, it's probably the rebel.

The point is this: we can literally "change our mind" by switching into a part of our brain that is appropriate for the situation we are facing. We can call on our adult mind to fill out the income tax forms. We can take a cue from the rebel when we need to blow off some steam—but do it in a healthy way. We can tell our toxic parent to take a hike when we find ourself using shame to manipulate our partner. These characters live in our imagination, but they are real—they have a history, body chemistry, emotions, thoughts, beliefs, and behaviors. They are the models of what we grew up with—the "committee," in recovery talk. As we change characters, as we choose these various aspects of self, we literally activate different thought patterns. As our thoughts and attitudes improve, interactions with our mate improve.

Spiritual Partnering

Intimate relationships offer the opportunity to heal our wounded parts—but not without some confusion. It's easy to think the other person is causing our reactions. And in a way, it's true—but only as a triggering mechanism. Triggers can be subtle, such as the way our partner enters the room, her tone of voice, a specific gesture, or an innocent comment that's the exact thing our mother used to say. When one of our own wounded characters gets revved up it's bad enough, but when it hooks into one of our partner's—and it usually does—you can imagine the chaos.

The psyche doesn't care about the details. If we have

unfinished business with a parent (and who doesn't?), the psyche will project the image of that parent on our partner's face, and we will react exactly as if our partner were our father or mother. There are no clocks or calendars in the subconscious mind. When the memory activates, it feels like it's happening now. We are no longer responding to the situation at hand but are in a regressed state of mind; we're in more than one time zone.

This dynamic becomes more confusing as our partner is triggered by our behavior and also regresses. There we are, a couple of seven-year-olds ready to duke it out! Or, with horns locked, we find ourselves in toxic parent mode. But at the same time, such a moment is an opportunity to heal a past wound. By recognizing each other's false ego states and saying a few carefully chosen words, partners have a very real opportunity to help create a different reality for each other. Responding sensitively rather than reacting in kind when a partner is in this regressed state literally changes the experience of the memory. It allows us to be intimately involved in each other's healing but without trying to fix each other.

Remember, we aren't analyzing each other's behavior, trying to solve something, or in any way trying to be each other's therapist. We are acting from our higher self, tuning into each other's spirit, reaching out a helping hand, being of service. Unconditional love is hard to come by, but understanding each other's inner world and responding lovingly comes close to that ideal.

Kinetta and Marc's Story Continues

Kinetta's father was a preacher who used shame as a way of instilling the straight and narrow in his congregation and his family. Kinetta hated her father's constant moralizing, so she was surprised (and confused) when she heard that same shaming tone in her voice when she talked to Marc. Rather than asking him to help her around the house, she would blurt out barbs such as "You're just lazy! If you expect me to do everything around here, you're just plain crazy!"

Marc would wince and duck behind his newspaper. He mouthed cusswords and even stuck out his tongue, he was embarrassed to admit later. The pattern was accelerating. They got locked into this scenario more often, and it took longer to break free. On the suggestion of a sponsor, Kinetta and Marc consulted a therapist, and they began to gain insight into their situation.

In therapy Marc revealed, "I know I'm acting childish, but I can't take her criticism." As they both talked they discovered that Kinetta's toxic parent triggers Marc's wounded child. Marc admits he shirks household chores—even though he's agreed to do them. He knows that his lack of responsibility is childish, yet he doesn't know "what comes over him." They also discovered that his irresponsible behavior sets off Kinetta's toxic parent. At one level they both see what they're doing, but once it reaches the tipping point, they can't stop.

Kinetta and Marc's mind game usually began at the dinner table. Kinetta usually cooked, and Marc cleaned up the kitchen—which he fully intended to do, but he often left the table as is and went into the other room to read the paper. He later admitted that he sometimes let the kitchen go until the next morning—and a few times he went to work leaving the dishes in the sink, but he had the *intention* of doing them. He said he wasn't sure if he did that to get at Kinetta, but it certainly had that effect.

Marc's procrastination threw Kinetta into her parental mode, and she resorted to shaming, as she learned at home from her father. This drove Marc deeper into his kid, and he hid behind the newspaper and made faces. Kinetta reacted to his behavior by becoming even more authoritarian. It wasn't working for either of them. Kinetta saw Marc draw away from her, yet believed reaching out to him would make her look *wrong*. With her "inner preacher" in control, looking wrong wasn't an option. Kinetta's body became as rigid as her attitude. Her breathing was shallow, her back and neck stiffened, and eventually she'd have a headache. Her toxic brain chemistry took twelve to twenty-four hours to work through her system. By then she'd be so invested in self-righteousness it would still be difficult to change her mind. Meanwhile, Marc had mentally stepped into an old battle with his mother and wasn't about to let it go. He was mad, his stomach in a knot. Likewise, it would take a day or two to burn off the toxic shame that was flowing through his veins.

Writing a New Story

With help Kinetta and Marc began talking about childhood— sharing the *feelings,* not just the story. As they saw how they were stepping into the past, they had a chance to react differently, and the healing process began. They had to learn how to stay in their recovered adult minds and have a healthy discussion about their situation. They accomplished this by beginning each problem-solving session with the Serenity Prayer. After a lively but not destructive debate, they agreed that an hour was long enough for relaxing after dinner before cleaning up the kitchen. Marc agreed to take responsibility, and Kinetta agreed to *not* remind him. She also surrendered her shaming pattern. In spiritual partnering, mates sign on to work on themselves, *with* each other—not work *on* each other. One little preposition makes a big difference.

Follow up: after several weeks both Kinetta and Marc became aware of other times when they slipped into the past.

They agreed on a phrase to call each other into present time: "I'd like to talk with your adult self, please." Tone of voice is key—the invitation must be offered in a higher-self tone of voice. Their willingness to work together to transform old patterns has drawn them closer and strengthened their marriage. They've become each other's greatest support system.

Transforming Love

The Big Book describes spiritual partnering this way: "If we have carefully followed directions, we have begun to sense the flow of His Spirit into us. To some extent we have become God-conscious. We have begun to develop this vital sixth sense." *God-consciousness* is the ability of partners to *recognize* (or "bring back to mind") each other's true spirit when they are unable to find it on their own. It's soul retrieval.

Here is an exercise to help you explore your inner worlds together using the ego states you've just learned about. These exercises develop self-awareness, and ultimately you gain more insight into the dynamics of your relationship. Avoid trying to do too much at any one time—slower means deeper. You'll continue to gain insights for a long time.

EXERCISES

Your Inner Parent

- What phrases does your inner parent use? (For example, "Don't make me stop this car . . .")
- What tone of voice does your inner parent use?
- What feelings do you have when your inner parent is in control? (Refer to the list in Appendix A if needed.)
- When is your parent most likely to take over?

- How does your partner feel when you're in parental mode?
- What are you feeling the moment before the parent takes over?
- Focusing on your answer to the last question, come up with a key phrase that will bring your higher self into mind when your parent takes over. For example, fear is a common trigger for a parental takeover. Consider a phrase such as "Everything's all right; we'll figure this out together," and see if it works for you.

Your Inner Child and Your Inner Rebel

Now repeat the same questions regarding your inner child and rebel states.

* * *

Recovery invites us to move beyond the deceptions and illusions of the past into present moment awareness. Our five inner "characters"—parent, child, adult, rebel, and higher self—give us ways of doing this by helping us see ourselves objectively; they offer perspective. As we get to know our characters, we become more compassionate and more loving toward ourself, which spills over into our partnership.

In the next chapter we'll discuss how that familiar reminder "HALT" helps keep us and our relationship on track.

Chapter Seven *

HALT: Recovery's Four Horsemen

There are plenty of unknowns in life and in relationships. However, many behaviors have predictable outcomes. We never, for example, outgrow the need for self-care—it's our primary relationship. A partnership can only be as healthy as the individuals in it. While we draw comfort and joy as well as other benefits from our relationship, we are responsible for our basic fitness. The Twelve Step program acronym HALT reminds us to not get too hungry, angry, lonely, or tired. Think of these as the four horsemen of recovery. Heeding their warnings can improve the satisfaction quotient in our relationship. Even more important, these *healthy horsemen* help reduce the chance of relapse. They can be built into your life together, giving you the best opportunity for a healthy, happy partnership.

ADDICTION NEVER SLEEPS

Most of us know the basics of a healthy life: three square meals a day, a good night's sleep, exercise, and a little fun on the weekend with friends. Add to that a full-time job, meetings, service work, prayer, meditation, child care, parental care, housework, yard work, and car maintenance, and top it all off with a committed relationship. Despite good intentions, HALT considerations quickly go out the window as we hunker down, just trying to get through another day.

The increased stress of today's world is creating health problems as well as marriage and family problems for the general population—and it puts recovering couples at greater risk for relapse. In relationships we tend to drift away from basic self-care, somehow magically expecting that love will take up the slack. *Yet relapse is the biggest single threat to our relationship.* Relapse begins long before "picking up" the substance. The downward spiral often starts by ignoring our health-maintenance plan, whose warning signs are known as hungry, angry, lonely, and tired. The quicker we interrupt the downward cycle, the better the chances of successful intervention. It pays to make HALT an integral part of your relationship health plan.

"H" Is for Hungry

We have a common need for healthy food at regular intervals, yet this simple task is not always easy to accomplish, particularly in recovery. If you are struggling with food, eating too much, not eating enough, forgetting to eat, or not eating the kind of food you need, you may need to talk with a health care professional, in addition to considering the suggestions in this chapter.

Food is complex. It nourishes the body, feeds the spirit, and makes us feel loved. It directly affects our physical, mental, emotional, and spiritual well-being. It seems like healthy eating *should* be easy, but it involves planning, grocery shopping, cooking, cleaning up—and then there is the matter of timing. Mates' busy schedules don't always line up. If kids are involved, there is another whole layer to consider. There are food preferences, special needs, and financial factors as well.

It helps if each partner takes responsibility for special food considerations. As for timing, it's best if we each eat when we need to, even if it limits eating together. However, sharing meals is important, too. It nourishes the spirit of the relationship. If we don't have time during the week, we can probably find time on the weekend to sit down together and make that valuable connection.

Nurturing the Spirit: What Feeds You?

Eating the foods that are right for us in the proper amount at regular intervals stabilizes our blood sugar, a major factor in smoothing out mood swings. Having an intimate relationship with ourself—let alone anyone else—is out of the question when we're bouncing off the walls one minute and depressed and angry the next. Not taking care of ourself at this elementary level keeps us, and our relationship, perpetually wrestling with unmanageability.

We make the connection between food and comfort early in life as we are held, cuddled, and fed in infancy. However, we receive nurturing in a variety of ways. Feeding our belly when it's our spirit that's hungry is scratching the wrong itch. In striving to feed emotional hunger, partners can overburden the relationship by relying too heavily on each other to provide all the nourishment their souls need. The Twelve Step program wisely emphasizes *fellowship*. Home group meetings serve us in many ways. The practice of getting together regularly, swapping stories, giving and receiving emotional support, and having a good laugh on a regular basis feeds our soul and nurtures our spirit.

Exercises: Feeding Our Body and Soul

A relationship calls for time spent together away from the world and also times fed by friends and new experiences. In a healthy relationship, mates find their balance point. Make a list of activities and places that feed you, and find time to connect with your "soul food" often. When discontentment, restlessness, or boredom begins to creep in, take time to identify what's going on, determine what can be done about it, and put it into action.

Food nourishes our body and soothes our emotions. We're using the term *home cooking* to describe meals that tend to both body and soul, making mealtime an event we look forward to. We may find that these added touches take more time and attention than we're used to, but that's the point. Remember, there aren't any golden arches over your table! You're turning mealtime into a total experience combining satisfying food, good conversation, and a pleasant table. This new attitude directly affects your relationship.

Recipes for Home Cooking

Food is sensuous—go ahead and *be* sensuous. Learn to eat slowly, savoring your food. After eating, linger at the table over a cup of coffee or herbal tea. Here are suggestions to help develop food consciousness and learn to enjoy home cooking together.

- Make food a primary focus. Because eating, health, nurturing, and sex are all part of the same equation, raising your food consciousness is integral to your love life.

- Learn about healthy eating. Get a couple of good books on food and nutrition, and read them together. Keep it simple.
- Collect recipes and create menus that honor both good health and food preferences.
- Take turns cooking, or cook together.
- Decide together on at least one time a week to share a meal together and treat it like a commitment—it is.
- You can pay a lot of money for ambiance in a fancy restaurant—but you can do it yourself for much less. Set the table using cloth napkins and make a simple centerpiece. Use flowers, shells, rocks, pinecones, vegetables, fruit, or pretty objects—include a candle and soft music. Get creative.
- Begin and end your meal with prayer—making it personal. Look at each other and tell your partner something that you are grateful for—such as, "I appreciate your positive attitude and the way you smiled when I walked in the door."
- Rule out using mealtimes for troubleshooting; make them about sharing positive thoughts or experiences you had that day. Troubleshoot only at pre-established times.
- Make an agreement to turn off the phones and television during meals.

The connection between food and sex is universal. All cultures have foods that are considered aphrodisiacs. Learn about them and include them. Remember, involve your imagination.

Talk about the results of your efforts. Has intimacy increased? Have tempers and moods evened out a bit? Do you want to eat together more often during the week? Are there any other changes that you need to address? If you or your partner resists making mealtime more nurturing, perhaps you need to cut back on your expectations. Sometimes less is more when making changes. Avoid forcing your partner into something; do a version of it for yourself.

"A" Is for Angry

In recovery we are warned against harboring resentments—and resentment is different than anger. Resentment comes as the result of not responding to anger when we have it; it's the backload of unresolved situations that fester and stew inside. Resentments are a leading cause of relapse.

Anger is a normal, healthy emotion indicating something's wrong. It's like a smoke detector telling us to pay attention—*to ourself*. Rather than taking anger out on others, we need to take the time to find out what's going on inside of us. Frequent bouts of anger indicate something is out of balance. Is there some way we aren't being fair to ourself? Are we expecting too much? Are we putting up with a situation that is actually intolerable? We might not be able to change the situation, but we can begin by telling ourself the truth. Whether it's a work-related issue or a relationship issue, acknowledging the problem opens the way for a creative solution.

Talk about it with your partner. If it involves something about your mate or the relationship, it might help to first sound it out with a sponsor or good friend. Suggestion: At Twelve Step meetings it's important to talk about what's going on with you, but it's not appropriate to talk about your partner's behavior. Talk about your personal relationship with a sponsor, close friend, or counselor, not at a meeting. When aggravating behavior continues, and issues don't get resolved, get professional help.

While anger is a normal, healthy emotion, it can lead to abusive behavior. It is never all right to take our anger out on others, either verbally or physically. Swearing, slamming doors, pouting, yelling, sarcasm, and making threatening gestures are toxic behaviors. It is possible to become addicted to our own adrenalin—it acts similarly to cocaine or other drugs that speed up our system. Once it gets into our body, it takes anywhere from several hours to several days for the chemistry to resolve, and meanwhile we're buzzing. Our heart is pounding, our ears are ringing, our blood pressure is soaring—our ability to make good decisions is rapidly declining.

Approaching a partner when you're angry isn't a good idea, although realistically, it may happen occasionally. But when anger becomes the defining tone, your relationship suffers and may not recover. Anger can be surreptitiously disguised as humor and used to back a partner off or "put her in her place" when you are uncomfortable. But sarcasm isn't honest. It will eventually drive a wedge in the relationship. Repressing anger is equally destructive. We can attempt to "manage" it by turning it in on ourselves, but that eventually creates health problems, not the least of which is depression. The bottom line is that anger is a helpful emotion but not one to act out or ignore. Use it as a signal, find out what you need to take care of—and take care of it. Here are three helpful things to remember about anger:

1. When we don't pay attention to our anger and hold on to it, it becomes resentment.
2. If we indulge in anger for the rush, it becomes addiction.

3. If we spew anger all over our partner, we become single.

Exercises: Befriending Anger

Treat anger as if it were your best friend telling you something for your own good. First, take the judgment off it and validate it. (Example: "For whatever reason, good, bad, or indifferent, I am angry.") Validation takes enough of the pressure off to give us a better chance at gaining insight. Check the other "horsemen"; they often ride together. Are you hungry, lonely, or tired? Write about your anger, talk about it with friends, share concerns at a meeting, or work with a sponsor. Sometimes talking with our partner about our anger helps identify what we're are angry about; but if you're angry *at* your partner and need to talk, do it *after* you've got a handle on it.

- Build a safety zone into your partnership: make it fair to talk openly about what's bothering either of you, with the understanding that it will eventually lead to a creative solution (but not necessarily in one discussion).
- Be able to tell the difference between working on an issue and beating it to death.
- Work together to learn more effective ways of problem solving—and practice them when you aren't angry. You'll find several processes for creative problem solving throughout this book.
- Our body gets mad when it's being driven too hard. Get real about time. Make a weekly schedule that includes honest estimates of travel time between appointments, meals, and other self-care that needs to be part of your day.
- Our body is our "horse." It needs to be outside

regularly and get plenty of exercise. Walk it around the block at least twice every day. Walk up a flight of stairs. We all know the health tips in the magazines—apply three of them. Keep it simple. We don't have to join the gym, buy gym clothes, bags, running shoes, hire a trainer, and so on. Just walk around the block.

- Keep track of our anger and notice what unreal expectations we have—about ourself, our partner, the relationship, job performance, the driver in the car ahead of us, and so on. It's often—maybe always—a case of unreal expectations.

- Use program principles such as taking another Fourth Step inventory to discover the deeper issues behind our anger. Being willing to make changes in expectations allows both partners to be comfortable.

"L" Is for Lonely

Loneliness is common human condition that reflects our inborn desire to love and be loved. We all need people, yet pairing up purely out of loneliness does not result in healthy partnerships. Relationships nurture us but aren't meant to fill us up—just top us off! We need to be able to count on our partner for support, but we can't expect a mate to regularly take the role of parent or caretaker. Recovery is about continued self-development. Part of that includes the ability to recognize our needs and meet them. We do that by leaning on the recovering community, friends, and family. And by finding our creative expression, developing hobbies, and pursuing interests. We can count on our partner for encouragement but not as a filling station.

Notice the word *one* in *lonely*. Sometimes when we're lonely we need to be with other people—but many other times we are longing for ourselves. It's another of those spiritual paradoxes. Are you spending enough time with yourself—doing things you love to do—or taking time out to do nothing at all? We lead busy lives. Trying to fit everything into each day, we may slice the bread too thin. Finding enough time for ourself and for a partner is challenging. As they say in the codependent recovery community, "Taking care of yourself is not an act of aggression against another person." But it can seem that way to a partner.

John Bradshaw voiced one approach to this mutual need for space: become "guardians of one another's solitude." Togetherness is important, and so is time spent with yourself—and it is possible to have both. Spiritual partners develop a connection that transcends personal wants. Respecting each other's need for privacy, for time alone, strengthens the bond and sweetens time spent together. There's a big difference between being guardians of one another's solitude and isolating or being neglectful. The needs of both partners have to be negotiated and sensitively met. Go slowly. It takes time to work these things out. Right now, know they can be worked out.

Exercises: Putting the *One* Back Into *Lonely*

- Practice being together while "doing your own thing." Design a quiet evening at home where you are each involved with a project, reading a book, or doing something you like to do, without relying on conversation or watching television.
- Go for a walk or a drive in the country simply commenting on the scenery, rather than having long discussions about other topics.
- Give yourself entire evenings without answering the telephone.

- Make it a practice for each of you to spend time with your own friends.
- Attend your own recovery meeting as well as one together.
- Enjoy an Explorer's Day Out (borrowing an idea from Julia Cameron's book *The Artist's Way*). Take an unscheduled day of exploring something interesting such as a country road, a great hardware store, a free day at the museum, or a meeting in another town. Just go wherever your curiosity leads you. No spending money: it's a look-but-don't-buy adventure. Share your discovery with your partner over dinner.
- Learn how to meditate and make it a regular part of your lives together. (Check the Resources list in the back of this book: try the CD *Six 11 Minute Attitude Adjustments*.)

"T" Is for Tired

It's possible to be really tired and to keep on going. When we've been depleted for a long time, we begin to accept feeling bad as normal. In the meantime, our immune system is out of whack and our mood isn't much better! Think dull, grouchy, complaining, and sick a lot. Not good relationship qualities. Chronic tiredness means we are running on empty, depleting our system faster than it is being regenerated. When this happens, partners will unconsciously pull energy from each other. No matter how much we love someone, if we are being drained by this negativity, we'll start pulling away or putting up walls of self-protection. If all this still hasn't made the point, consider that when we're tired our sex life suffers!

The T in HALT officially stands for *tired*, but can also

stand for *thinking*—as in "stinking thinking." Sleep studies at the University of Minnesota Medical School indicate that any amount of sleep deprivation diminishes mental performance, impacting our ability to think and reason appropriately. In simulated driving tests, participants who missed a night's sleep performed as poorly as drivers with legally intoxicating blood-alcohol levels.* Sleeplessness for an extended period of time indicates a physical or emotional situation that needs investigation. Loss of sleep can end up in active addiction.

Sleep is nature's Step Two—it restores sanity! It reverses the symptoms mentioned above, promotes sound judgments and good decisions, and improves performance at all levels. It creates a positive state of mind and stabilizes mood swings. Sleep helps normalize an uneasy nervous system, a common result of addiction that can continue to be a problem years into recovery. Sleep renews our spirit, repairs ourbody, stabilizes emotions, and refreshes the mind. It is essential in healing traumatic memories. We need to sleep deeply enough and long enough to pass through our entire dream cycle. We process our emotions and gain wisdom and understanding through dreaming, whether we remember the dreams or not.

Crowded work schedules and other commitments intrude on the time we need to spend together to maintain our connection—and they get in the way of enjoying cuddling and sex. On a given day, sharing a bed may be the only time we spend together. It's challenging to catch up

---

*Source: Mahowald, Mark, quoted in "The Effects of Sleep Deprivation," available at http://www.familymatters.tv/level_4/health/sleepdeprivation.html

with the news, solve problems, have sex, and still have time for a good night's sleep. Yet without logging the recommended sleep hours, the energy to enjoy life isn't there.

Exercises: Sleep Is the Best Bedtime Story

Chronic tiredness can indicate a condition that needs medical attention. By all means, begin by consulting your health care professional. Consider your diet: you may not be eating enough energy foods—raw fruits and veggies—or maybe a food intolerance is slowing you down.

If tiredness is interfering with your relationship, consider the following suggestions:

- If you are tired from working too much, investigate the appropriate Twelve Step program.
- Include exercise in your daily schedule. Walking assures better sleeping, but walk early in the day or early evening, not just before bedtime.
- Treat your bedroom as sacred space, and avoid taking problems to bed with you (this isn't referring to your partner, however).
- Attend to the basics of good sleep: dark room, cool temperature, no television, and comfortable bed and bedding.
- Eat your last meal by six o'clock and have only a light snack if hungry at bedtime. Include a relaxing cup of chamomile tea as part of your bedtime routine.
- If either of you is too tired for sex at night, consider sleeping first and having sex in the morning.
- Six deep belly breaths induce relaxation—practice deep breathing with a tape or CD. Or consider deep breathing together before going to sleep.

- If snoring or any other physical or emotional problem is causing sleep problems, get help—sleep is necessary for your relationship to thrive.

IMPROVING THE ODDS

Most of us have to make a living, and we enjoy our busy lives. But recovery principles insist that we consider our mental, physical, emotional, and spiritual well-being along with our other obligations—and that includes partnerships. As adults we are responsible for meeting our essential needs—*that's the rule.* If our foundation wasn't secure in childhood, building it will be like putting a basement under the house after it's been built. (And you've been living in it for how many years?) It's going to require additional effort, but can be done—carefully, one cinder block at a time.

* * *

Couples in successful relationships are able to sustain equilibrium through the normal chaos of living and ride out the occasional storms. This takes the presence and participation of both individuals. Working together means offering each other support as each tends to his or her own basic needs. You can build a self-care program into your relationship. And remember, when you are having problems with your relationship, consider your HALT program first.

Next we'll take a look at gender differences, hopefully separating some of the myths from reality.

Chapter Eight *

Gender: Friend or Foe?

Who would suspect that one tiny little leg on a chromosome could make such a huge difference? Yet a fractious bit of DNA is all that lies between life as an XX woman or XY man. It calls the gender shots, designating the hormonal composition of every single cell in the body and fashioning the uniquely different structures of the female and male mind and body. The shorter way of saying this is that men and women are different.

Perhaps it was another piece of the American dream struggling to be born that turned our assumptions about male and female roles upside down in the 1960s, or maybe it was one too many Hepburn and Tracy films. Some folks trace the shift back to Rosie the Riveter, the World War II symbol for women putting on the pants and going to work in the factories. Rosie did her part for the war—while singlehandedly turning the apron into a museum piece. Regardless of where the first battle of the sexes was waged, gender differences came under serious fire during the last century, challenging the established order of business.

As in many other social movements, when these issues

came "out of the box" they came out for good. Now we see their effects on our language: for example, *he* is no longer the inclusive term it once was, and we've learned to say *he or she* when appropriate. We've grown accustomed to gender-neutral terms such as mail carrier, flight attendant, and councilperson. Changes in the workplace have affected the home front, too. In many two-income households, partners split housekeeping, and it's not unusual to hear of stay-at-home dads.

As society's rules shifted and women—and men—struggled to adapt, gender differences were minimized. Especially in competitive fields, women entered the system by striving to be *like* a man, not different from one. Now, in the wake of Title IX, affirmative action, and other gender-conscious legal struggles, men and women stand before a court of law equal in every way—and it's become okay to look at differences again. Today, different does not imply "less than" or "wrong."

Gender Wars: Waving the White Flag

The differences between male and female are organic; the *significance* assigned to innate differences is a matter of culture. We can make light of gender differences: think of those frantic escapades on TV's *I Love Lucy* when Lucy and Ethel put one over on Desi and Fred. Such stories make for good comic relief. For most of our history, however, gender differences have had serious social effects. Men have been in charge, making the decisions at all levels of society, including the family, and women have not always been happy about it. This imbalance is adjusting. The new paradigm is one of partnership and mutual decision making. As it emerges, it challenges traditional marriage. Many say that things ran smoother in the "good old days," but running smoothly isn't always the highest value, particularly when it is accomplished at the expense of others' pursuit of fulfillment.

Complementary, Not Competitive

Today the trend is toward seeing gender identities as complementary aspects of the human psyche and valuing equally what each brings to the table. It's a human tendency to fear what is unlike us. Men and women can seem to be very different creatures. But nature has taken care of business, and within the psyche of each male there is a bit of female, and inside of every female is a bit of male. It assures that the genders can relate to one another well enough to form lasting emotional and physical bonds—thus assuring the continuance of the species.

We talk about coming to terms with our opposite nature and developing our full personhood. As a man becomes conscious of his feminine side, his male characteristics will still continue to dominate; he will remain true to his essential male nature. His self-assuredness, along with his instinct to protect his home and provide for his family, will remain intact. At the same time, he will get in touch with his intuitive, relational side. The opposite is true for a woman. Her more receptive feminine nature will remain primary, but she will balance caretaking, for example, with taking care of her own needs. Her essentially relational nature will make room for her individuated sense of self. As we make peace with our opposite nature, we become more peaceful within ourselves, and our relationships with the opposite gender improve.

The Inner Marriage

Jungian analyst Marion Woodman, among others, cautions that we can't hope to love the opposite sex until we meet and fall in love with the opposite aspect in our own nature.

Through a process known as the *inner marriage*, we bond with our inner "mate." As we experience our own opposite gender, we gain insight into its true meanings. The inner marriage brings balance and security to the psyche. It prepares us to find our mate and marry for love and appreciation of one another's differences: not as two halves becoming whole but as two whole people living and loving together—full partners with the ability to honor and benefit from each other's wonderfully different ways.

The terms *male* and *female* pertain to energies or qualities that are the product of hormonal differences and result in physical, emotional, and mental characteristics. Within each gender, huge differences exist that are the composite results of this biology, along with social conditioning and personal choices that affect how individuals express their gender in the world and in relationships. For the most part, couples in same-sex partnerships demonstrate the same dynamics as heterosexual couples; one person often expresses the feminine and the other the masculine.

There are times and tasks every day when we draw on our opposite nature. Women are outgoing, brave, protective, and, according to the old song, can bring the bacon home and fry it, too. Men defy the limits imposed by traditional society and raise babies, teach school, are nurses and cooks, and excel at homemaking. The main point of this discussion is to appreciate the differences in gender regardless of who is expressing it or how.

Gender is more than *what* we are. It is *who* we are, and inner marriage or not, men and women can never completely understand each other. Opposite genders can't fully get inside the other's psyche—they aren't intended to. They cannot see the world entirely from the other's viewpoint. But it is important to appreciate the differences. The mystery of gender is the dance of opposites that keeps love alive!

Richard and Maria's Story

Richard had a particular gripe about Maria: whenever they were preparing to go somewhere, it took her forever to leave the house and get to the car. He complained about her disorganization, even accusing her of deliberately stalling to make him angry.

Richard talked with his sponsor, who asked him to examine his ideas about men and women. "Why do you start from the belief that your need is more important than hers?" He suggested that Richard do a Fourth Step on his attitude toward women and, in the meantime, politely ask Maria to help him understand what took her so long to leave the house. When he did, he was amazed at her answer.

Maria told him that she always went into each of the children's bedrooms as well as their own, blessing the space and saying a prayer of safe return. She confided in her husband that while she knew she had to encourage her children to explore the world, she also worried about the dangers they encountered every day. They had many important decisions to make about drugs, alcohol, sex, and other behaviors for kids not yet in their teens.

Richard felt his heart open. He was engulfed in a feeling of love and appreciation for Maria and the care she gave to their family. He asked her why she had never told him. She said she didn't think he would understand, being a man! From then on they gave each other a few extra minutes and both of them performed the leaving-home ritual and walked out to the car together.

GIRLS AND BOYS

Males and females tend to score equally on intelligence tests, but the way they think and solve problems is different. In his popular book *The Wonder of Boys*, Michael Gurian makes one of those huge oversimplifications that perhaps we can get away with once in a while. Gurian says that men are about moving objects in space, and women are about relationships. This can be seen early in childhood, as girls are far more likely to choose dolls, while boys will go for toys with wheels or propellers. His book, along with other scientific studies, confirms what parents have long known—boys and girls have different behaviors, and the differences are obvious early.

Snakes and Snails and Puppy Dog Tails

Testosterone, a man's dominant hormone, shapes his body, mind, and spirit. His body is wired for a cycle of building physical tension followed by a sudden release of it. It gives him his muscle mass, his love of competitive sport, and his vigorous sex drive. It provides the male with his assertive spirit and penchant for risk taking. A boy will show early signs of independence—listening less to voices around him and preferring to follow his biological urge for adventure, expansion, and exploration (translation: he won't stay in the yard). Nature wires the male brain for spatial logic—and with a fascination for moving objects through space. Boys are drawn to technology and building. For the most part, they are linear thinkers, excelling at creating systems. Males are programmed to move quickly and solve problems; they have the ability to focus and get a job done. Men's innate skills have helped shape their role in the society as explorers, inventors, builders, protectors, and providers.

Sugar and Spice and Everything Nice

A preponderance of estrogen shapes the female body, mind, and spirit, giving girls a nesting instinct and receptive natures. Females' physical bodies and emotions go through distinct changes throughout the month, giving her a cyclical nature. Women are caretakers. Needing and seeking connection, they make efforts to understand others. Women are skilled at language and also with the nuance of communication: perceiving and interpreting tone, inflection, facial expressions, and emotions. Her brain is wired for women's intuition. Her sense of adventure is internal—pulling her inside herself where she explores her own inner landscape and seeks to understand herself and the human psyche. Women's wiring has given them the edge in managing family relations and as society's natural diplomats. They are able to see multiple sides to an argument and perhaps respond with more accurate empathy than their male counterparts. This gives them the advantage in big-picture decisions.

Honoring the Mystery

Many of us have acquired a host of preconceived false ideas of what all men are like, or aren't like, or of what all women can and can't do. These notions limit the human spirit—ours and our partner's. If you have been raised to be suspicious or disrespectful of the opposite gender, your relationship will reflect this discord. Life is riddled by contradiction; it's often a study in opposites. The truth is that partners are mirrors of each other's mental and spiritual condition. We come to terms with ourself, our lover, and others through acceptance. In time we encounter all aspects of being human—success lies in embracing it all.

Gender differences deserve to be celebrated. Male and female *togethering* is the creative impulse of the universe. Men and women can bring out the best in each other, and they do that on a regular basis. However, gender differences can also become destructive. We have the ability to turn each other into the enemy—to focus on that which is naturally and purposefully different and make it appear to be strange, beyond comprehension: that is, totally unacceptable.

Questions We Have about Our Mates

Despite all the research and theories, and despite giving acceptance our best shot, gender differences still bring up a lot of questions and more than a little head scratching. Let's look at some typical questions that come up in our daily lives.

Questions Women Have about Men

What's with the channel surfing?

Men's eyes are wired for short, quick glances and scanning space. He's using the skills needed to spot dinner running through the forest, but now they're converted into channel surfing and video games.

Why does he act like he can't hear me?

There's a good chance it's not an act. Vision is man's best sensory skill. Your guy doesn't differentiate the background noises as much as you do and doesn't sort through it to find *your* voice as well as you would like him to. Think of it as *focusing* rather than ignoring you.

How is it that I'm writing a research paper, cooking dinner, and listening for the baby and when I ask him to answer the phone he says, "I can't, I'm fixing the back door"?

Men are linear thinkers. When they are on a task, they lock into it and don't want to come up for air until the job is done. Let the machine answer the phone.

Why can't he just listen to my feelings?

Men have more wiring in the part of the brain that relates to spatial concepts, and are not as interested or adept with emotions as women. However, they are very good at solving problems. Maybe that's why your guy tends to downplay your tears in favor of getting to the point and solving it logically. It can be helpful if you tell him when you just want him to listen while you express yourself; you don't need him to solve anything for you. And also let him know when you *do* want his help.

Can't he ever just cuddle?

For men, sex is primarily a biological event. An innate ability allows them to separate sex from emotions. And their natural tension and release cycle prepares them for a quick sexual encounter. Men need to—and will—learn a slower, more emotional, sensual, approach to satisfy a woman. But you need to understand that it isn't necessarily his natural way: *he's doing it for you.*

Questions Men Have about Women

Does she think I'm a mind reader?

Many women have trouble asking for what they need—and often they don't know. They're good caretakers for others but not always so good at taking care of themselves. Sometimes they can tell you exactly what they want and other times they look to you to figure it out. Probably the best tactic is a light intervention with the suggestion she sit down and tell you what's going on—even when you already know.

Why does she want to know what I'm thinking about?

Women's brains never turn off. They are programmed to keep up with everyone's emotional state, constantly reading and interpreting people's cues. It's different for men: your brain is "on" when you're focused on something; otherwise it's got a screen saver. This isn't about intelligence—it's about economy. When women can't pick up any signals from your facial expression, they feel like it's their job to ask. Of course, they *need to* (and will) learn to respect your privacy, but they'll probably still want to know.

Can't she understand how much I hate those "talks?"

Go back and read the previous answer and realize that she probably does know how much you hate those talks. Women are about keeping peace in the nest. When she has a complaint, she's usually hoping to make everyone's life run smoother—and you need to be open to hearing it. It is rare for women to powerbroke in relationships. However, they can learn that saying "Honey, we need to have a talk" can turn even the bravest man into a plate of jelly. They can learn how to approach you with care.

Why can't she move on and "get over it?"

Women can get heavily dosed with estrogen, particularly at certain times of the month, which generally correspond with you wishing she'd get over it. If women designed the world, they would lounge on the sofa and eat bonbons for two weeks out of the month and work double time the other two—that's how they're wired. If they have to maintain a constant schedule day in and day out when their body clock says rest and regenerate, women can become moody, ill-tempered, even depressed. You might want to be her hero and help her get the extra R & R she needs.

Can't we just have sex?

Women have to feel close before having sex. Men feel close *by* having sex. Sometimes a woman will have sex with you to accommodate you, but if it's really about getting close, she needs the romancing—the ritual. Read on to the next chapter.

Toward a Vision

Society is always changing, and change carries with it confusion, fear, and resistance. Despite the shouting and the claw marks, change is constant. Our recovery gives us the choice of consciously participating in how these changes unfold. The dawn of the third millennium invites us into more conscious and respectful ways of relating.

How we work through gender differences affects more than just our own relationships. Harmony between partners is reflected into the world—it contributes to peace on the planet. One of the ways the Twelve Step community carries the message is through inclusive communities where men and women form close personal friendships, listening and learning from each other. We all need to be recognized and accepted for who we are. When we accept each other at the level of gender, we are touching the core. By knowing our differences and accepting our natures, we not only become better partners, we become better human beings.

EXERCISES

With your partner, use these questions to help you explore your attitudes and beliefs about gender.

- What are three things you each love about your own gender?
- How were gender differences handled in your home when you were growing up?
- Notice areas where you and your partner can turn your natural differences into complementary roles. What is necessary for that to happen?
- What behavior or attitude does your partner have that is difficult for you? Can you imagine accepting it? Can you imagine appreciating it? If you could, how would it feel? How might that change your attitude?

- What ideas or attitudes about gender do you hold that might limit how you relate to your partner?
- What gender restrictions have you placed on yourself?
- What are three behaviors or attitudes your partner has that you find fascinating?

* * *

Gender differences are real—they're supposed to be. The fact that men and women are different isn't a problem; it's the value we place on the differences that get us into trouble. The movement today is toward seeing gender as complementary rather than competitive aspects of humanness. However, we all know that the path of true love isn't always a smooth one, and it helps to know how to handle disagreements in a healthy way. In the next chapter you'll read about sex—that "mighty urge," as the Big Book describes it. You'll also read about the spirituality of sex and find out what "really real" sex is all about.

Chapter Nine *

Sex, Spirituality, and Satisfaction

The impulse to procreate may be the primal force behind sex, but that alone doesn't explain its power. Sex ignites the imagination; it has spawned music, art, and libraries of literature. On its sunny side, sex arouses romance, passion, rapture, and love. It makes us want to slay a beast and lay it at our lover's feet. But its dark side can harbor pain, anguish, betrayal, and even violence. It can make us want to slay our lover and lay him at the beast's feet. The book *Twelve Steps and Twelve Traditions* tells us sex is a gift from God, "a creative energy that deeply influences our lives." We deserve to enjoy a vibrant and satisfying sex life, yet many things get in the way.

Qualities such as honesty, honor, self-awareness, healthy self-esteem, equality, free choice, emotional intimacy, affection, and the capacity to give and receive—combined with that most mysterious ingredient, sexual attraction—ideally result in a healthy, happy sex life. But some folks, through no fault of their own, have complications that interfere with forming a satisfying sexual relationship. In his book *Sexual Anorexia*, Patrick Carnes describes the two phenomena of sexual anorexia, or the avoidance of sex, and sexual addiction, or an out-of-control need for sex. Both are used to manage painful emotions.

Within the bell curve of human sexuality, anorexia and addiction would represent the extremes. Our discussion will focus on the range of sexual behaviors in the middle range considered healthy.

Sexuality: Many Variables

Individuals have different sex drives, which vary at different times. We have periods of high sexual energy, others when we aren't as interested, and times when we don't feel like having sex—all within the normal range of human sexual behavior. Extended periods of abstinence from sexual relations in a marriage or committed partnership are not rare. However, prolonged loss of sexual energy may indicate problems that need to be addressed medically or psychologically.

The natural ebb and flow of our sex drive is affected by our health, energy level, demands of children and other family members in our care, work schedules, anxiety and depression, medication, and addiction, including addiction recovery when other priorities can require all our attention. In addition, there are psychological and social factors such as the rules we grew up with, religious restrictions, abuse, inexperience, and bad information about sex. With all the variables, it's almost impossible to imagine that each partner's sexual energy would always match exactly.

A healthy, vibrant sex life can enhance the quality of our relationship. Likewise, the quality of our relationship influences our sex life. Generally speaking, a sex life alone won't sustain an unhappy relationship. Sex seldom solves our deeper problems, but it can provide the safety and comfort that holds us together while other matters are addressed, as long as they are being addressed. This can happen by actively working a program that addresses the concerns in the relationship, working with a sponsor, including a marriage sponsor, participating in Recovering Couples Anonymous, or seeing a counselor.

Some Common Questions

For all the buzz, we have some very distorted ideas regarding sex. Each day we are exposed to more information bites on the topic—and not only information, but *advertising*. Media minds know that sex sells, and super-sized sex sells more. So a highly inflated idea of sex has become the cultural norm. Paraphrasing the Rolling Stones: *a lot of useless information,* and *I can't get no satisfaction!* And then consider addiction, and the years a person can spend distorting sex through drugs, alcohol, and other substances. Whether you are in recovery or not, the questions are many. For example:

What about having sex when one of the partners isn't all that into it?

There are those occasions when all possible factors converge exactly right for a nearly perfect sexual encounter, and there are other times when we settle. Obliging our lover when we don't really feel like making love, and agreeing to other encounters of the quick kind, can be both satisfying and passionate—or it might be ho-hum at times. Either way, when done as a free expression of love, it works. Pressuring a mate or submitting when we don't want to isn't healthy. Being a couple doesn't guarantee sex on demand. There are times when we don't want sex with our partner for a variety of reasons—and it doesn't call for medical or psychological attention. Chronic discontentment or disappointment in other areas of our life can get misdirected at a partner or the relationship (the "I'm with the wrong person" syndrome). If you're going through one of these episodes, take time to find out what is underneath your disgruntlement. Frustration, restlessness, and dissatisfaction can indicate the start of a relapse cycle or a bout of "stinking thinking." They can also indicate that the antsy partner needs to get to the gym more regularly. Sometimes we just get on each other's nerves.

What do we do when work crowds out our love life?
If work seems to be ruining our sex life, whether we're overtired, we work opposite shifts, or we work late hours, the first thing we need to do is get our calendars out. We need to line up times when our schedules give us enough time together so we'll feel like making love. If we're overtired, we can consider napping—together, if possible. If work has us going opposite directions all the time, consider shift changes or even employment changes. Putting our sex life (and our partner) on hold indefinitely can be the undoing of a relationship. Changing jobs is probably easier than changing partners. Nonetheless, under some circumstances we are doing everything we can to keep our heads above water financially, and sex simply isn't our main concern. This can work on a temporary basis, but if it's a pattern, consider job counseling and working with a sponsor.

What do we do when kids interfere with our love life?
When children are in our life, it's often a case of *get it while you can.* Imagination fired by desire yields surprising results. Quickies in the bathroom with the door locked, trading child care with another couple, or occupying the children with TV cartoons or a favorite DVD are only a few suggestions. One couple said they occasionally sneak out to the garage and have sex in the back of the car while the kids

watch TV. Far from feeling deprived, they say it rekindles the passion of their courtship. The simplest solution might be the best: put a lock on the bedroom door.

How about chronic tiredness and general disinterest?

In chapter 7 we noted the importance of self-care in a relationship. Health and well-being have a direct effect on our sex life. When disinterest in sex persists, partners might want to talk about what's going on and perhaps seek help. Sometimes being comfortable in your relationship morphs into sloppiness and sex appeal suffers; other times more serious concerns such as depression are involved. It might be uncomfortable to talk about, but when weighed against our partner's health or a lost love life, we might find the words. A weekend away with the intention of rekindling our love life can work, but it needs to be mutually agreed on—and planned together. Surprises further destabilize a wobbly situation. It's best to check to see if our partner wants to address the problem. In the meantime, sexual energy is creative energy, and we can direct it in other ways. We can pursue other interests such as art, music, or a sport, or take an interesting class. But chronic dissatisfaction with our sex life, despite attempts to get help, can be a deal breaker for many couples.

What happens when previous sex abuse or rape interferes with our relationship?

Being in a sexual relationship is often the trigger that brings up repressed memories of abuse. Memories might surface through sexual activity as we recall specific events, possibly traumatic ones, and re-experience those emotions and physical sensations. The memories might make us apprehensive or fearful about sex; they might precipitate disinterest, avoidance, or even feelings of revulsion. The memories themselves aren't dangerous, but they can feel very threatening; untreated, they can trigger a relapse. When memories resurface it is a time of healing, although it doesn't feel that way in that moment. Previous sexual abuse, rape, or other issues of physical and emotional abuse need to be addressed with a professional. Partners can play an important part in healing one another but need information and support to do it. We can begin by attending Survivors of Incest Anonymous meetings or checking the resources in the back of the book.

What happens when a partner is unfaithful?

Infidelity causes a serious break in trust in a marriage or a committed relationship. What constitutes infidelity can depend on the agreement a couple has made. But the term itself implies sexual transgression with another person. When it has happened, counselors as well as sponsors have different opinions regarding full confession between partners. Following the directive of Step Eight, we might consider whether these circumstances might cause unnecessary suffering. Consider the length of time since it happened and the frequency—was it a momentary lapse or a pattern? Was it part of active addiction which was then followed by real healing? Other therapists say exactly the opposite—that it must be disclosed to a partner in all cases. Either way, if there is any chance of having exposed a partner to disease, the infidelity must be made known regardless of the other factors. It's a good idea to get help with this, as it can ruin a marriage either way—by telling and by not telling. Partnerships that survive infidelity usually grow stronger.

What happens when one partner is a flirt or hints at wanting sex with others?

Flirting is natural, however, it is also confusing and can cause hurt feelings all around. It's a kind of socially acceptable sexual acting out. It's risky behavior. It's not necessarily dangerous—but it can be. If our partner is doing the flirting, we can ask our partner to help us understand his or her reasons for it. Flirting can be a substitute for more honest conversation by a person whose communication skills are weak—he or she might not know how to have a conversation with someone for whom there might be an attraction. Sometimes it's just playful, and if it isn't causing anyone any problems, there isn't a problem. If we are doing the flirting and it's causing our partner concern, we might ask ourselves why we do it. Sooner or later the idea of having sex with someone else occurs to almost all of us. We don't have to act on it. In recovery we talk about "thinking the drink through" to its logical conclusion. That can work for infidelity, too. Some people feel a partner's emotional intimacy with another person can be more threatening than sexual intimacy. As noted earlier, what constitutes straying depends on the terms of your agreement, and our agreements need to be honored. If either partner wants to change the rules, it constitutes breaking an existing agreement and making a new one. Most of the time that doesn't work.

What about a partner who is sexually repressed or inhibited?

This is often the result of family programming or religious beliefs. We can encourage each other to share our stories using the kind of the questions found in the exercises throughout the book. For example, how was sex discussed in our family? Family and religious conditioning can usually be successfully addressed within the marriage between two sensitive people. If this doesn't resolve it, we might seek professional help.

What about impotence?

Begin with a physical check-up. If that doesn't address the condition, look into the emotional factors. Impotence doesn't have to mean no sex. Consider practicing non-genital sex, where the point is pleasure but not intercourse or orgasm. Holding, kissing, light touch, and massage awaken pleasure receptors. Take turns practicing giving and receiving. Impotence isn't always permanent. Some couples say that caressing and nurturing each other can be as pleasurable as sexual intercourse and often restores sexual power. Taking the focus off genital sex helps get past the problem when it isn't an irreversible medical condition.

What about partners who can't talk about sex or tell a partner what they want?

Sometimes words are overrated. Begin by showing your partner what you want. Place your hand over his or hers and lightly guide your partner. Respond by sighing or by physical gestures when it feels good. Touch yourself where you want to be touched. Some couples like to use technical terms for body parts and techniques. Others prefer pet names, innuendo, or insinuation. Almost all couples develop a private love language and affectionate names, which can make talking about sex easier when you're shy about it. When there is a real reticence or fear to consciously engage in sex, partners would benefit from professional counseling.

What happens when one partner likes sexy movies and the other doesn't?

Some marriage counselors recommend that couples watch erotic movies together as a way of revitalizing their sex lives. It can stimulate the imagination and help partners break free of old restrictions. Others talk about the negative results such movies have on the sex lives of the couples they counsel. What makes one kind of "dirty" movie good medicine and another destructive to a healthy sex life? Both porn and erotica show sex in explicit ways, but what differentiates destructive pornography from "fun and games in the bedroom" is the *mutually seductive* factor. In order for it to qualify as erotic, both partners who are watching have to be aroused. Erotic material shows satisfying sex between equal partners—it's arousing, not destructive. Pornography is objectifying and derogatory—it promotes power abuse through sex and is destructive to the human spirit. Unfortunately, truth in advertising doesn't apply in this arena and the labels don't differentiate the content. It's easy to tell the difference within a few minutes. If either partner has a problem with it, it's not good medicine.

FIVE SUGGESTED ESSENTIALS FOR HEALTHY SEX

In identifying what is meant by a healthy sexual relationship, marriage and family therapist Wendy Maltz sums it up this way: Healthy sex is characterized by consent, equality, respect, trust, and safety, or "CERTS," as it is known. Here, her model is adapted to incorporate Twelve Step wisdom.

- *Consent* means consciously giving permission to engage in sex free of coercion. This involves the full consent of both people. Coercion includes attempts by either partner to control the relationship through sex—insisting on sex or withholding it, perhaps using "moods" to prove a point. It includes freedom from the influence of drugs and alcohol. Recovery is based on free choice, and the same is true of your sex life.

- *Equality* makes consent possible. Equality means partners are equal in the relationship—drawing their personal power from whatever divine source they imagine, not from each other. In recovery terms, this is a partnership in which partners neither dominate nor become dependent on each other.

- *Respect* comes from valuing each other's full personhood. It begins with a positive regard for ourself and our partner both in and out of the bedroom. It includes qualities such as consideration, thoughtfulness, celebration of each other's uniqueness, and a sense of reverence for each other.

- *Trust* means feeling physically and emotionally safe with our partner. It implies that both of us can risk vulnerability and count on our partner's sensitive response. It involves honoring each other's boundaries and at the same time being willing to experiment together. We can't practice trust with people who are untrustworthy—honesty is key.

- *Safety* means being safe and comfortable about when and how sexual intimacy takes place—it implies that partners are making choices together. Both feel free from the possibility of harm, including unwanted pregnancy (this applies to men as well as women), sexually transmitted disease, and physical injury. This means being conscious and clear-headed enough to make responsible decisions regarding birth control and condoms.

These qualities lay the foundation for healthy sex. They create an environment where a full range of healthy behaviors and emotions can grow. Loving couples enhance their sex with affection, romance, intimacy, sensuality, playfulness, and much more.

The Oxytocin Connection

In one sense, sex can be seen as a series of biological events primarily focused on reproduction, mainly about how to get a sperm and egg together. But that's a far cry from the "mighty urge" for the fullest possible union described in *Twelve Steps and Twelve Traditions*. Recovered sex involves our whole being—spiritual, mental, emotional, and physical. We are sensate little creatures from the moment of birth. We crave the touch of skin on skin and comfort of our mother's breast. We hunger for food and the touch of another person. Without human contact we will quickly perish. The more we are touched, held, and cooed at, the more we thrive.

Oxytocin, touted as the love chemical, is supplied in the womb, and babies get more of it as they nurse. It's the feel-good chemical that fuses nurturing, pleasure, and relationship in the brain for life. It becomes the blueprint for loving, nurturing sexual relationships. Our own body produces this important hormone though out life, and men and women release it during sexual orgasm. The deeper, more lasting peace described above isn't as likely when sex is limited to intercourse; it's the relational aspect of it—the affection and nurturing—that releases its full power. Sex includes every interaction between mates: how you engage over morning coffee, the look in your eyes as you go your separate ways in the morning, a quick call during the day—every thought you have about your partner belongs to the mating dance. Sex between committed partners doesn't guarantee full satisfaction every single time, but it holds the potential.

Toward a Spirituality of Sex

Sex opens the heart, strengthens bonds of love, and nourishes us on many levels. The deepest kind of sex has a transcendental nature that puts us in touch with the sacred. Sex that is truly connected to our spiritual center lifts us out of the everyday world and transports us to mystical or supernatural realms. Set free from ordinary time and space, lovers enter into deep communion with their own soul essence, with one another, and with divine essence. In sex we merge into an orgasmic sense of union. The experience proves to our doubtful mind that separation is an illusion. We seek union. It is the transcendent quality of sex, its mystical nature, that fuels the search. What we seek, God is.

"Really Real" Sex

Modern religion divided creation into two separate realms—one for the sacred and one for the profane, the profane encompassing all worldly things, including you and me, and definitely including sex. While this is the view that most of us grew up with, it wasn't always the way things were perceived. For most of human history it was commonly believed that the entire cosmos was alive with sacred presence. Divine beings regularly romped and mated in nature—sexuality and the spiritual life were entwined and encountered everywhere in every aspect of life. Many cultures still hold this view.

Philosopher Mircea Eliade describes this awareness of spiritual presence as an encounter with the "really real." Using his phrase, spiritual sex is *really real*. Its really real nature is rooted in our own center and springs from the freedom of living by internalized spiritual values—beyond laws and rules imposed by others. That means letting go of old ideas, ones that don't truly reflect your sensuous nature, and surrendering to love. Sex is the connection between beloveds, and it symbolizes their love and connection to God.

Yes, but will it last?

We're feeling the heat of passion now, but what about the

future? Relationships go through phases, and therapist and lecturer Terence Gorski identifies them as *infatuation, power struggles, safety/security,* and *ebb and flow.* Infatuation is that time of attraction and courting when passion runs high. Infatuation is followed by a time of tumult where passion seems to turn against us, expressing itself mainly through power struggles. Couples who make it through that difficult time ease into a period of safety and security. This is followed by a time of ebb and flow, of rediscovering each other and falling in love all over again

EXERCISES FOR BOOTING UP YOUR SEX LIFE

Healthy sex between partners is characterized by playfulness and willingness to explore the limits. The following exercises are designed to gently push those limits. Sometimes one partner is feeling more adventurous and wants to try something new, while the other isn't so sure. Relationship is about allowing someone inside your boundaries—and allowing yourself to change the "rules." Be creative, have fun, give things a try. Relationship is a place where fantasies can come true. Here are a few suggestions to get you started.

Preparing for love: A slow, sensuous preparation for lovemaking enhances the experience. A bath or shower, followed by lotion or oil, a clean shave, a hint of perfume or cologne, can add to your sex appeal. If it makes you feel sexy, it will add to the experience.

Connecting breath: Breath is your vital force—the living spirit within you. Begin lovemaking by breathing slowly and deeply together for several minutes. Draw your partner's essence into you. Look into each other's eyes, and be grateful for this moment. Deep breathing together allows your spirits to blend. It slows the mind down and awakens your senses. It is relaxing and stimulating at the same time.

In praise of passion: Praise each other lavishly. Both men and women need and love to be admired. Create love language. Find words and phrases that please your partner and apply them generously. Read love poetry to each other, slowly and with passion.

Change the scenery: Making love in different places and at different times of the day or night increases passion. Make love on the floor, the couch, outdoors. Change your love-making time—try making love in the morning, noon, afternoon as well as night.

Squeezing the juice: A lot of the fun is in anticipation. Rather than a surprise evening or weekend away, go for the carefully thought-out one. Spontaneity is fun, but planning an evening away together, selecting just the right place, gown, music, candles, and flowers, adds juice.

Call me in the morning: Anytime your bodies are close, your brain is making those love chemicals. Cuddle on the couch while watching television or reading. Avoid always having sex at night if you're tired. It's better to go to bed early, get a good night's sleep, and make love in the morning.

Fantasy rules: Women—Ask your guy what he likes you to wear to bed. What makes you feel sexy will usually work for him, too. Consider a slow, tantalizing strip tease with music; try "The Stripper." Men—Ask your lady what she likes you to wear to bed. Some like their guy nude; others prefer a tee shirt and shorts look. One man keeps a hard hat and tool belt in the closet as per his mate's request.

The slow burn: Allow passion to heat up for several days before making love. Whisper sexy incantations to each other about what you're going to do—but no following through until the third night.

Dirty dancing: Sexy dancing used to work when you were dating, and it probably still does.

Sex is nourishing: Combine food and sex, and get creative. Don't forget the raspberry drizzle.

* * *

Sex is a natural instinct, a gift from God, according to *Twelve Steps and Twelve Traditions.* Healthy sex is entered into freely with full, conscious consent of both individuals. It is based on mutual respect, trust, and safety. Sex bonds us as partners and holds us together as a couple during difficult times. It offers the most pleasure when it is in the context of relationship, rather than an isolated event. Sex opens our heart and nourishes our spirit. Its transcendent nature is physically pleasurable and spiritually fulfilling. Sex is such an important part of a couple's life together that if we're having difficulty we deserve to get help.

Next we'll consider how couples and families cope with the results of addiction and the challenges of recovery.

Chapter Ten *

Help for Nonaddicted Partners

Addiction is a family disease. The Big Book, in the chapter "The Family Afterward," recommends that the newly recovering mate be greeted with generous amounts of tolerance, understanding, and love. That sounds good in print, but mustering up those qualities is difficult in the aftermath of addiction. Family dynamics have changed, altering family structures and expectations in a big way. Bill W., cofounder of Alcoholics Anonymous, was ten years into sobriety when his wife, Lois W., founded Al-Anon, the group for family and friends of substance abusers. Perhaps that fact sheds a little light on her experience of living with a recovering alcoholic.

Before treatment we may have lived with a partner who was angry, manipulative, irresponsible, and got stopped for driving intoxicated one too many times. Or maybe our partner was a jolly old soul with a beer in hand whose liver started to fail. Whatever our circumstances, once our partner enters treatment, we feel relief. A burden has been lifted and we're moving forward. After our partner goes through treatment, the ball bounces back to our court—now *we* have to do the work of forgiving and moving on. Once again, our partner's problem is our problem. How do we ever get past the resentment?

The recovering person faces many struggles in confronting the inner demon of addiction. Behavior is erratic as moods rise and fall in the midst of this chaos. Maybe our jolly old soul's mood has turned sour without alcohol: he now has an edge to him, a mood that's dark and somber or nervous. We liked him better when he was drinking. Our angry wife has mellowed, but she can't seem to stay focused, she cries at the drop of a hat, and she's gaining a lot of weight. Her interest has shifted from drugs to ice cream, which she definitely prefers to sex. Our situation doesn't seem to have improved—it's just different. We see that the task of rebuilding almost every aspect of life is before us. Meanwhile, the reality of relapse looms in the shadows.

Where's the joy in all this? The needs of the recovering member often conflict with the needs of the nonaddicted partner, and adjustments have to be made and prioritized. We have to radically adjust—sometimes entirely let go of— hopes, dreams, and expectations as we address changes in the family structure and chart a new course. The Big Book offers encouragement in describing recovery as a journey from maudlin sympathy and bitter resentment to a state that is happy, joyous, and free. But it doesn't offer a timetable.

The First Step in a Long Journey

It's impossible to avoid getting emotionally involved in a partner's addiction and difficult to avoid taking responsibility for his or her recovery. There's so much riding on it.

Experience has proven that spouses have as little control over a partner's recovery as they had over the active addiction. Tiptoeing around to avoid upsetting the apple cart, rescuing, and making excuses are all counterproductive. Recovery hinges on the addict or alcoholic taking responsibility.

We feel pain and frustration as we stand by and watch someone we love caught in the disease. We've survived by denying our own problems and the disease's personal effects on us, but it's catching up with us. The best thing we can do is get into recovery ourselves and to get help for other family members.

Recovery for partners comes in the form of Al-Anon, a Twelve Step group for the loved ones of addicts. Al-Anon teaches acceptance, but acceptance doesn't mean settling. It means getting a clear handle on our situation and following a course of action guided by hope, not driven by fear. Sometimes right action means doing nothing, but not the frozen kind of doing nothing; it's more like a peaceful surrender and the serenity it brings. Working a Twelve Step program, going to meetings, spending time with a sponsor, and getting additional therapy if needed provides encouragement for the journey. As we develop new life strategies, we realize that we don't have to keep stepping in the same pothole. We can choose to walk around it.

Priorities for Partners

Recovery for nonaddicted partners happens through the process of learning more about ourselves: who we are, what we want and need, our hopes and dreams. And it means letting go of attitudes and behaviors that get in the way of doing that. Twelve Step recovery is a group effort. Following are issues that other partners have faced in healing addiction as well as suggestions on how they handled them.

Safety First

Personal safety is the number one priority. If the addict was violent toward family members when using, family members may be unwilling to allow the recovering addict back in the home right away. Trust has to be reestablished, and that will take time—and lots of it. Both partners need to understand how long the trust-building process can take and understand their role in it. If the violent behavior was addressed during treatment, the perpetrator should be in an aftercare program that addresses domestic violence. In the case of sexual abuse, the recovery time for survivors is longer, and many counselors don't believe there is a compete rehabilitation for perpetrators. Getting continuing professional help is vital. Programs and counseling services are available through social services in most communities.

Find a Program

When the newly sober partner walks in the door, the journey to recovery has just begun. It's going to take time for the family to reorganize and heal. Children's needs must be met first, and that can mean that the nonaddicted partner must continue to shoulder more than a "fair" share of responsibility for some time.

Finding the right program can help the nonaddicted spouse and other family members sort through feelings: consider attending meetings of Al-Anon, Codependents Anonymous, or Adult Children of Alcoholics.

Eventually, issues of power and decision making as well as financial matters will be addressed, but perhaps not in the first stages of recovery. Sharing responsibilities and establishing a process for decision making will be gradual. Being the responsible one, yet not treating our partner as an irresponsible kid, is a delicate balancing act but a necessary one. Recovering families often say that the hardest challenge they faced was the recovering person's need to spend precious time away from the family—going to meetings and working with others. There is no quick solution, and it's helpful for the recovering person to hear *firsthand* (at a meeting) how others have done it.

The Guilt Trap: Out, Out, Damned Spot

Guilt is paralyzing. Lady Macbeth demonstrated its insidious nature when she struggled in vain to wash her hands of it. (Of course, she really *was* guilty!) Feeling guilty when we take a day off, or sit down and rest, or do anything nice for ourself doesn't make sense, yet we allow ourselves to feel that way. We sometimes lump a lot of negative emotions together and label the whole mess as guilt. We apologize, and apologize, and apologize, but it doesn't budge. When the feeling of guilt doesn't go away even when we say we're sorry, we probably haven't done anything wrong. Guilt keeps us from taking positive action to make our life better. It's a trap. The best way to get rid of it is to surrender it. Write it on a piece of paper, put it on your altar, burn it, bury it, ask your Higher Power to come and get it, but in some way symbolize getting rid of it. Then remove the word guilt from your vocabulary. Look at the feelings list in Appendix A of this book, pick a few feelings you'd rather have, and talk about them.

Frequent Check-Ins

Feeling like there is enough time for everyone and everything is tough. Taking thirty minutes during each day to check in with a spouse is helpful. While all issues can't be resolved during this time, it's a pressure release valve. One recovering family spends thirty minutes in a family circle after dinner. Each person checks in, reporting what has gone well and what he or she is fearful, worried, or angry about. They observe the "no cross-talk" rule, listening but not commenting. Unless something obviously needs immediate attention, all concerns are acknowledged and briefly noted in a family journal. The meeting concludes with the following prayer: "God, you have heard the concerns of each member of this family. We affirm our love and support of each other and place ourselves in your hands. We gratefully accept our continued healing." While going to Twelve Step meetings is necessary, making time for family is an important part of recovery, too. Now look again at the first sentence in this paragraph and realize what a great job you're doing—especially if you don't think you are.

Reckoning with Relapse

Addiction includes the potential for relapse, but with time and as the recovering person gains new skills, the success rate for recovery improves. As mentioned earlier, relapse begins long before the user picks up the substance again. An obvious indication that the cycle has begun is that the recovering person starts missing meetings or otherwise abandoning the recovery program. Other healthy routines may break down as well. Lapses in self-care such as forgetting to eat regular meals, abandoning an exercise program, missing work, and skipping out on chores or other commitments are warning signs. Mood swings, sleep disturbances, and poor thinking begin. Emotional barometers include frustration, anger, depression, anxiety, guilt, shame, despair, compulsiveness, and nervousness.

The sooner a relapse cycle is recognized and addressed, the less likely it will result in using. Partners are often the first to recognize changes in their loved one's behavior. There is a gnawing temptation to resort to patterns of the past: enabling, denying, or trying to control the situation. Honest feedback can make a difference in interrupting the cycle but is seldom the deciding factor. Responsibility for behavior and keeping on track with recovery always remains with the recovering person—it's what makes it work.

One woman talked about watching her husband's behavior change over a three-week period. She was able to simply tell him she was observing an old pattern and that it concerned her. He asked her to describe his behavior more specifically. She was able to offer factual feedback, saying he had missed his regular meeting two Saturdays in a row and also cancelled a regular basketball game with friends. She reported noticing his growing frustration, specifically cursing and rude driving. Her ability to relate what she saw with objectivity and precision was a skill she learned in Al-Anon meetings. He realized he was drifting into dangerous waters and accepted his wife's intervention, seeing it as her concern for him. Her detached yet caring approach gave him the space he needed to assess his situation without feeling that she was taking over and telling him what to do.

When a Breakup Is Inevitable

Sometimes, regardless of everyone's best efforts, partnerships fail and families split up. *Get help before making permanent changes.* This in no way commits you to staying or leaving, and it can make either outcome less destructive to all involved. Regardless of the circumstances, breaking up is painful and affects the whole family. It can trigger relapse for you and your recovering partner. Stepping up your support program is strongly recommended. Allow a cooling-off period, and avoid moving ahead too fast and making important decisions when you are upset.

Laura and Frank's Story

Laura and Frank lived on a small horse farm outside of Louisville, Kentucky. They were married for five years when Frank's cocaine use got out of control. Frank was a veterinarian and a highly respected person in the horse-oriented community where many relied on him to keep their valuable racehorses healthy. He was surprised and embarrassed when the sheriff knocked on the door and arrested him. Laura was relieved.

Laura had spent too many nights alone, frightened, and angry as her husband's addiction drew him away from home and into a world she feared. Frank was mandated into a six-month recovery program for professionals, and Laura marked the days off on her calendar. She had hopes of getting her husband back and dreamed about the life they could have together. When the day finally arrived, their reunion was strange. He seemed distant, and she felt rejected. About thirty minutes after getting home, Frank left for his NA meeting and didn't return until nine that evening.

Frank soon settled into taking care of his practice during the day and going to meetings every night. He developed a whole new community of friends that Laura didn't know and didn't feel welcomed in. When she expressed her disappointment at not spending more time together, Frank became defensive. She cried, stomped her feet, and threw things, but nothing changed. She threatened to leave, but quickly took that off the table as she pictured the reality of heading out on her own.

Laura called a friend who she knew was in Twelve Step recovery, and they talked for a long time. The result was that Laura started going to Al-Anon meetings and began her own recovery. The key phrase she recalls was her friend's comment "You don't have to live like that." She was surprised to realize how much she relied on Frank for her happiness, and how much of her energy went into caretaking him. It wasn't easy, but two years later, Laura went back to school to complete her education. And in a few more years she had a job as a translator in a global company. Before recovery she wouldn't go anywhere without Frank, and now she travels worldwide on her own and with friends, and occasionally with Frank. She laughs as she admits her basic tendency is still to pull back inside herself and to expect Frank to do "it," whatever it was. That was the way it worked in her home, and it had been her pattern for a long time. Today she smiles easily and is sure of herself. If Al-Anon had posters, Laura could be its poster child.

Practicing Principles in Family Affairs

Children who have been living with an addicted parent have lived in chaos. And the chaos doesn't just suddenly straighten out and go away when the parent gets clean and sober. Reorganizing the family will require a new game plan. Principles create order without attempting to cover every possible situation with a rule. Teaching kids principles gives them a way to think their way through decisions that fall outside the rulebook. Remember, each generation invents a new version of reality; they're supposed to. Rather than being one step behind our kids, we can give them the tools they need.

We can use the principles presented here as a starting place. As your family develops its own list, post them on the wall or refrigerator door. Seeing the list creates safety and order at home the same way it does in a meeting room. Principles have endless interpretations and applications and can become the focus of many interesting dinner conversations. We need to be sure to *listen* to our kids, as they struggle with decisions using principles. Remember, we maintain authority, guiding them but not taking over.

Principle: This is a family whose members are present and support one another.

The values expressed here are commitment and endurance. Today, blended families are the rule, not the exception. Many relationships include kids—and the "yours, mine, and ours" scenario is not uncommon. Relations between stepparents and stepchildren can be challenging. Different histories, different child-rearing philosophies, and different hopes and dreams for the future have to be blended. Relations among siblings are complicated. It all takes time and careful attention. Terms like presence, support, commitment, and endurance impart hope and the understanding that relations can improve through patience and participation.

Principle: This is a family that practices love, compassion, and forgiveness.

The values expressed here are tolerance, acceptance, trust, and the strength of the spirit. Imagine how different our life would be if our parents had taught us to forgive and forget. We have the chance now to change a family pattern and probably live to see it in our grandchildren. When our kids need forgiveness, give it to them upfront (fore-give-ness). Avoid bringing up past mistakes—yours or others'—even in a kidding way. Make the consequences of their behavior about learning a lesson rather than earning forgiveness. That's how you stop passing along the guilt.

When making amends to your children about your own past, keep it sincere and short. Leave details and specifics out of the discussion unless they bring them up. Be ready to listen if they have more to say, but avoid going back over a laundry list of your shortcomings. *It's about them now, not us.* They are much more in the present moment than we are, and they forgive and forget as soon as we take responsibility. Going over the story drags them through the past. It's self-indulgent, and it burdens them with our guilt.

Raising kids is about letting them get on with their lives. We're the railroad station, and they're the train passing through, headed wherever. We lay the tracks, and we give them as much information as we can about what lies ahead, but we won't be on the ride with them. They do best when the tracks are clear and straightforward as we can make them, and when we don't overload the train with our stuff. They need to know we're there, taking care of ourselves, so they don't have to spend precious energy doing that.

*Principle: This is a family in which everyone's voice is
          heard and valued.*

The values expressed here are communication, respect, listening, and self-esteem. Keep the communication lines open—*both ways*. Talk to your kids, and spend twice as much time listening (the one mouth, two ears equation). Ask them questions, but don't confuse questions with interrogation. Good questions help children develop insight. Invasive ones make them clam up! Parents tend to take over the conversation, telling their children what they're supposed to think rather than hearing what they are thinking, and helping them explore options.

It's natural to want to protect our kids by giving them the answers to life. Take a moment and remember how we reacted to that one! Using principles gives children moral reasoning skills. It builds trust and lays the path for them to come to you when they need help. It builds the framework for future decisions that they'll have to make on their own. Think of the most effective sponsoring you experienced.

Try some responses from the list below to encourage conversation. Practice them in everyday situations and then, when something bigger is at stake, the thoughts and words will be there.

- That's interesting. Can you tell me more?
- What did you do next?
- How did you think of that?
- What a creative idea!

- That sounds challenging. Keep me up on how it goes.
- I know you, and I know you are a smart kid. I know you'll find a really great answer.
- I can't wait to hear what happens next.

Some situations require a stronger approach in parenting. It is possible to get through them with much less resistance when reasoning and problem-solving techniques are in place. You have the last word both morally and legally, but be careful not to squander your authority. They'll withdraw or rebel. Try these responses when you need to maintain the power of parental veto without squashing.

- I can see you feel very strongly about that, and I do too. We'll need to talk more.
- I am not comfortable with what you're telling me you've decided. Let me hear how you got to that decision.
- I'm sure we can find a solution that works; we just haven't gotten there yet.
- Can you tell me what principle you are using in this decision?

EXERCISES

Getting Rid of Guilt

First ask yourself some questions.

- How long has the guilty feeling been with you?
- Have you carried it far enough?
- If not, how much longer do you think you need to carry it?
- How is it serving you?

Now imagine how you would feel if you didn't feel guilty. Write down at least three feelings. And ask yourself if it's all right for you to have them and ask for them in your prayers.

Next, substitute one "G" word for another. Rather than saying you feel so guilty (for having a nice day) say you feel grateful. This really works.

Finally, stop apologizing unless you have actually committed a felony!

Exploring Values

First, ask yourself these questions.

- What values did you learn in your family of origin?
- How did you learn them?
- Are these values you want expressed in your family today?

Now spend some time with your partner identifying important values you want to express in your family. Next, talk about specific ways these values can be expressed in the family. Write them down and post them on the refrigerator door.

* * *

Dealing with addiction is hard, yet many couples are successfully facing the challenges, maintaining sobriety, and finding happiness. No one's story is exactly same, but the problems and solutions are similar. Use the information in this chapter as a starting place and explore options—including finding the right program for your particular circumstances.

Next you'll find some handy tips and suggestions to help when your relationship needs a quick tune-up. You'll also discover how sponsorship played a vital role in one couple's marriage.

Chapter Eleven *

Reminders, Handy Tools, and Sponsorship

There are no quick fixes in recovery, but we can use some simple reminders, learn some new tools, and take advantage of more support. This chapter offers a little of all that and a story of how one couple's marriage has survived thanks to a sponsor's good advice.

SHOW A LITTLE R-E-S-P-E-C-T

We want to be comfortable together, but we can cross the line and take each other for granted. We can sometimes overlook the many little ways we can nurture each other and feed the spirit of respect in our relationship. The following suggestions are ways we can show consideration to our mates as individuals, as well as partners—it all adds up to respect. We can:

1. Pray and meditate together to help foster the spiritual in our relationship.

2. Include our partner in our Tenth Step and make apologies quickly.
3. Be willing to forgive and forget.
4. Be affectionate. Say I love you often. Smile, hug, and hold hands. Kiss each other hello, good-bye, good night, and whatever else we can think of.
5. Speak respectfully about our partner to friends and family, and respect our partner's family and friends.
6. Respect each other's privacy, and keep confidential matters confidential.
7. Acknowledge that we need time together in our relationship and time alone—be willing to make adjustments until we find our right mix.
8. Keep the spirit of curiosity alive in our conversations. We can be interested rather than threatened when we encounter a different idea or opinion. We can always learn something new from our partner.
9. Mind our manners—please, thank you, and excuse me count.
10. Accentuate the positive. We all complain to our partners about work or family or other things, but we can still keep the scale tipped toward positive interactions.
11. Cultivate the attitude of gratitude about each other and express it often.

Keep It Light!

Laughter is good medicine! It offers perspective. Humor has lasting emotional and physical health benefits—and relationship benefits, too. Here are eight things laughter can do for us, for our health, and for our relationship.

1. Reduce stress and tension.
2. Stimulate the immune system.
3. Increase natural painkillers in the blood.
4. Decrease inflammation.
5. Normalize blood pressure.
6. Lift our spirits.
7. Strengthen a bond.
8. Keep our relationship fresh.

MORE QUICK REMINDERS

1. *Make a new life.* We have the right to make our lives work for us.
2. *Rewrite family history.* You have the pen, write a new chapter.
3. *Set new boundaries.* Old behaviors cannot be extinguished and reinforced at the same time. It may be necessary to limit interactions with our family of origin while we install a new program.
4. *Find new models.* Notice couples who have what we want and hang out with them. Learn what they do and how they do it. They provide models while we design our version of healthy relationship.
5. *Think new thoughts.* Patterns are neuro-pathways in our brain. They will eventually close when we don't use them, so if you don't indulge an old attitude or belief, it will go away. In the mean-time, when the neuron fires in our head (the old impulse), we have to take it in a new direction. Interrupt "stinking thinking" and think some-thing nice. We're creating a new pathway in

our brain. At first our new messages may not feel true, but say them or act on them anyway.

6. *Say new words.* One woman changed the impulse to put her husband down by saying "How come out of all the guys in the world I got the best one?" Her guy's smile lit up the whole room. She was so surprised at his reaction that she became a believer!

7. *Embrace new habits.* In recovery we live by spiritual principles, not old laws. It is the up-to-the-minute instruction booklet we've been looking for.

Boost Your Laugh Quotient

Humor happens. We experience it in recovery meetings when people honestly share their story or talk about their day. As others connect with the experience there is spontaneous laughter. Genuine humor—not joke-telling—is natural. Here are ways to add humor to our life.

- Notice humorous moments that naturally happen all around us every day.
- Share an amusing thing that we observed or that happened to us today.
- Watch funny movies.
- Reflect on good times we've had together. Humor doesn't have to be the knee-slapping variety to lift the spirit. Couples who can laugh at themselves or at their situation usually feel stronger when problems arise. Laughter can sometimes release negative tension both physically and psychologically.

Bless Our Home

Creating a home together is more than just having a roof over our heads; it's a tangible reflection of our commitment. We can bless our home through a personal ritual of our choosing. We can spend some time talking with our partner about what we want our home to reflect and then set that intention consciously. Light a candle, burn incense, express our gratitude.

Ideas for honoring our space:

- Manage television time and make conscious decisions about how much and what we watch.
- Plan at least one evening at home together as a family each week where we turn off the phone and the TV.
- Keep our space orderly and clean. Practice simplicity—avoid clutter and pass along things we don't need rather than stuffing them into closets.
- Decide on the guidelines together regarding who is invited into this space, how often, and when.

Stake a Claim on the Holidays

For many recovering people, holiday memories are anything but happy. We might find ourselves trapped in traditions that are destructive or have no meaning. And some of us may have grown up with no experience of celebrations.

Reclaiming the holidays is important to developing a sense of family—and it's fun. At the same time, changing holiday rituals can spark the sense that we're tampering with things we shouldn't be messing with. But we have the right to make our lives work for us. Setting boundaries is part of becoming a family unit, and we've earned the right to create holiday experiences that express the spirit of recovery—happy, joyous, and free.

Seven Tools to Use Instead of Losing It

1. Take a deep breath. Take another one.
2. Work your program: pray, meditate, call your sponsor, go to a meeting, work a step—any step.
3. Go for a walk.
4. Ask yourself, what is the most loving response in this situation?
5. Let your partner know you'll talk later when you get a handle on your feelings.
6. Write about it.
7. Read "Acceptance Was the Answer" on page 417 of the Big Book (fourth edition), or better yet, have it laminated and post it on your refrigerator door.

From "Acceptance Was the Answer"

And acceptance is the answer to all my problems today. When I am disturbed, it is because I find some person, place, thing, or situation—some fact of my life—unacceptable to me, and I can find no serenity until I accept that person, place, thing, or situation as being exactly the way it is supposed to be at this moment. Nothing, absolutely nothing, happens in God's world by mistake. Until I could accept my alcoholism, I could not stay sober; unless I accept life completely on life's terms, I cannot be happy. I need to concentrate not so much on what needs to be changed in the world as what needs to be changed in me and in my attitudes.

CONSIDER A RELATIONSHIP SPONSORSHIP

Tom and Annie's Story

Tom and Annie had been married for two years when Annie started a new life in AA. Tom was confused by the changes in her and in their relationship. The party doll he married suddenly got serious, reflective, and *spiritual*. They were struggling with their marriage and close to breaking up when Tom found Al-Anon. He was soon going to meetings several nights a week and running with a whole new crowd. Now Annie's hackles went up, but she had enough recovery to know not to interfere with Tom's program. Her recovery wasn't delivering the promises—yet—and her marriage was not offering any solace either. She spent many hours contemplating leaving Tom.

It was then that Annie heard a woman named Rhet speak at a meeting about her thirty-year marriage. It reminded Annie that a lifelong marriage with Tom was what she wanted more than anything. She asked the woman if she would become her relationship sponsor. Rhet accepted, and together they struggled their way through the Steps, this time applying them to Annie's marriage. Before they talked, however, Rhet insisted that Annie write about any disagreements she had with Tom. Rhet's first question to Annie always was: what are you getting out of the fight? Was she getting power from being right, or sympathy by being a victim, or energized from the adrenalin rush of the battle? "The power is on your side of the street," was Rhet's constant reminder. Annie recalls her sponsor's words: your partner's actions might be annoying and even unacceptable, but the *power is in choosing your reaction.*

Annie learned that she could change her feelings by changing her thoughts—something that hadn't occurred to her before. As her thinking became more flexible, situations weren't as black and white as she had thought. They could be interpreted many different ways. While it's normal and healthy to have a reaction to our partner's behavior, getting stuck in it builds resentment; it holds us back. Annie learned to write about her reactions and talk about them with her sponsor until she had a handle on them. As her emotions settled down, she almost always saw the situation differently.

Annie realized there are things we have to accept in a partnership if we want to stay together. And there are changes we can make regarding our own expectations, tolerance, patience, and love—but she couldn't always do it. There are also times when a partner's behavior is unacceptable and needs to be addressed, but not in the heat of battle or from the level of emotion. Staying on our side of the street includes asking ourselves what we need to do to take care of ourself, and doing it. That's something we can't do effectively when we are reacting to a person or situation. Annie got better at it.

Rhet was adamant about the principle of acceptance, saying, "Insight is on our side of the street, and insight ultimately leads to wisdom." Annie tore page 417 out of her Big Book and had it laminated. But she wasn't ready to surrender that final "gotcha," and neither was Tom.

After three years of weekly face-to-face conversations with her sponsor, along with countless phone calls, Annie threw in the towel and ended the power struggle that threatened to bring down her marriage. One morning as she was jogging in the park, the miracle hit her like a bolt of lightning. After three years of weekly conversations with her sponsor, along with countless phone calls, Annie "got the message." She realized the battle would end when one of them quit fighting. She threw in the towel and ended the power struggle that threatened to bring down their marriage. "When I surrendered I totally felt like a winner," she said. The dynamic with Tom quickly changed. His attempts to engage her didn't get a nibble. Annie found her freedom and a new happiness—most of the time.

About six months after waving the white flag, Annie called Rhet with the news that she and Tom were expecting a baby. Anna Marie's birth was followed a few years later by brother Ben's arrival. Tom got a sponsor and reinvigorated his Al-Anon recovery.

Tom and Annie are proud of the work they've done together, but the marriage is seldom smooth. Both strong-willed individuals, they are still learning how to work together. Today she sees that power has a thousand faces. Power issues can crop up not only around important decisions, such as those affecting children, but also around topics as trivial as what brand of mustard to buy. Annie believes that without a recovery program and her sponsor's support, she and Tom would have given up their marriage before giving up their death grip on control. She is grateful for the family they have together and for the ongoing support of her sponsor. Annie says they're making progress and she's let go of the idea of perfection—at least for today.

Recovering Couples Anonymous

Couples seeking support for their partnership can contact Recovering Couples Anonymous (RCA) at its Web site, www.recovering-couples.org, or at its Oakland, California, office: 510-663-2312. Couples sponsorship is available, as well as many other resources. If there isn't a local chapter in your area you can join an online group. RCA members also hold a weekly teleconference. Other online resources offered by RCA include couple agreements, stories, helpful lists, tools, daily reflections, and more. Contact information and a complete catalog of services is available at the Web site noted above.

Recovering Couples Anonymous offers these promises. *

If we are honest about our commitment and painstaking about working the steps together, we will see these gifts in our lives:

Our love will flourish as we experience mutual forgiveness.

Trust in each other will return.

We will learn how to play and have fun together.

We will be better partners, parents, workers, helpers, and friends.

No matter how close to brokenness we have come, we will be able to help others by sharing our hope, strength and experience. Just as our love for our partners has been imperfect, we may not always be adequately able to express to you the deep love and acceptance we feel for you. Keep coming back! The process of loving and communication grows in us and with each other one day at a time.

* * *

As we have seen, relationships are rewarding and challenging. They are hard work but well worth it to many couples

---

* Recovering Couples Anonymous World Service Organization, "The Gifts of RCA," available at http://www.recovering-couples.org/ vision.php. Reprinted with permission.

who are learning how to do it one day at a time. Recovering relationships are about making the conscious effort to be together and maintaining the willingness to learn new skills. We deserve to get as much help as we can in doing that. Many of us have found that support by working our recovery program and applying it to our relationship. Finding a relationship sponsor can put the third leg on that stool.

Afterword

The Big Book reminds us that there are no accidents in God's world. We've come together for the purpose of working on important spiritual issues, and that can take time—even a lifetime. Relationships call for patience, understanding, self-reflection, hope, lots of love, and more. When we choose to live our life in a close personal relationship with another person, we commit to being spiritual partners—allies on the journey. By accepting and loving ourself and our partner as we are, and accepting and valuing our partnership as it is, we take the first step in nurturing the qualities necessary to allow it to become all it can be.

The spiritual journey is one of self-discovery. Relationships offer us the chance to know and be known intimately. Through the mirror of relationship, we come to terms with the hidden parts of ourselves, and in this way become whole.

Appendix A *

Feelings Inventory

Being able to express exactly how we feel helps us in the on-going process of self-discovery and enriches our under-standing of and deepens our connection to others. The following are some words that express a combination of emotional states and physical sensations.

How we feel when needs are satisfied:

Affectionate	*Confident*	*Engaged*
compassionate	empowered	absorbed
cozy	open	alert
friendly	proud	curious
loving	safe	engrossed
open-hearted	secure	enchanted
sympathetic	solid	entranced
tender		fascinated
warm		interested
		intrigued
		involved
		lively
		spellbound
		stimulated

Excited
amazed
animated
ardent
aroused
astonished
dazzled
eager
energetic
enthusiastic
giddy
invigorated
lively
passionate
vibrant

Exhilarated
blissful
ecstatic
elated
enthralled
exuberant
radiant
rapturous
thrilled

Grateful
appreciative
moved
thankful
touched

Hopeful
expectant
encouraged
optimistic

Inspired
amazed
awed
full of wonder

Joyful
alive
amused
delighted
glad
happy
jubilant
pleased
tickled

Renewed
enlivened
refreshed
rejuvenated
rested
restored
revived

Serene
accepting
balanced
calm
clear-headed
comfortable
centered
content
fulfilled
mellow
peaceful
quiet
relaxed
relieved
satisfied
still
tranquil
trusting

How we feel when needs are not satisfied:

Agitated	*Anxious*	*Depressed*
alarmed	cranky	dejected
discombobulated	distressed	despairing
disconcerted	distraught	despondent
disturbed	edgy	disappointed
perturbed	fidgety	discouraged
rattled	frazzled	disheartened
restless	irritable	forlorn
shocked	jittery	gloomy
startled	nervous	heavy-hearted
troubled	overwhelmed	hopeless
turbulent	restless	melancholy
full of turmoil	stressed out	sad
uncomfortable	tense	unhappy
uneasy	uptight	wretched
unnerved		
unsettled	*Confused*	*Disconnected*
upset	ambivalent	alienated
	baffled	aloof
Angry	bewildered	apathetic
enraged	dazed	bored
furious	hesitant	cold
incensed	lost	detached
indignant	mystified	distant
irate	perplexed	distracted
livid	puzzled	indifferent
outraged	torn	numb
resentful		removed
		uninterested
		withdrawn

Embarrassed
ashamed
chagrined
flustered
guilty
mortified
self-conscious

Fearful
apprehensive
dread-filled
mistrustful
panicked
petrified
scared
suspicious
terrified
wary
worried

Frustrated
aggravated
annoyed
discontented
dismayed
disgruntled
displeased
dissatisfied
exasperated
impatient
irritated
irked

Grieving
agonized
anguished
bereaved
devastated
heartbroken
hurt
lonely
miserable
regretful
remorseful

Hostile
contemptuous
disgusted
hate-filled
horrified
repulsed

Tired
beat
burnt out
depleted
exhausted
fatigued
lethargic
listless
sleepy
weary
worn out

Vulnerable
fragile
guarded
helpless
insecure
leery
reserved
sensitive
shaky

Yearning
envious
jealous
longing
nostalgic
pining
wistful

Appendix B *

The Twelve Steps of Alcoholics Anonymous*

1. We admitted we were powerless over alcohol— that our lives had become unmanageable.
2. Came to believe that a Power greater than ourselves could restore us to sanity.
3. Made a decision to turn our will and our lives over to the care of God *as we understood Him.*
4. Made a searching and fearless moral inventory of ourselves.
5. Admitted to God, to ourselves, and to another human being the exact nature of our wrongs.
6. Were entirely ready to have God remove all these defects of character.
7. Humbly asked Him to remove our shortcomings.
8. Made a list of all persons we had harmed, and became willing to make amends to them all.

---

* The Twelve Steps of AA are from *Alcoholics Anonymous,* 4th ed., published by AA World Services, Inc., New York, N.Y., 59–60.

9. Made direct amends to such people wherever possible, except when to do so would injure them or others.
10. Continued to take personal inventory and when we were wrong promptly admitted it.
11. Sought through prayer and meditation to improve our conscious contact with God *as we understood Him,* praying only for knowledge of His will for us and the power to carry that out.
12. Having had a spiritual awakening as the result of these steps, we tried to carry this message to alcoholics, and to practice these principles in all our affairs.

Resources

Suggested Reading

Alcoholics Anonymous: The Big Book, 4th ed. New York: Alcoholics Anonymous World Services, 2001.

Beattie, Melody. *Beyond Codependency: And Getting Better All the Time.* Center City, MN: Hazelden, 1989.

Borysenko, Joan. *The Power of the Mind to Heal.* New York: Bantam, 1988.

Bradshaw, John. *Creating Love: The Next Great Stage of Growth.* New York: Bantam, 1994.

Carnes, Patrick. *Out of the Shadows: Understanding Sexual Addiction.* Minneapolis: CompCare Publishers, 1983.

Faulkner, Mary. *Easy Does It Dating Guide.* Center City, MN: Hazelden, 2004.

Gorski, Terrence T. *Getting Love Right: Learning the Choices of Healthy Intimacy.* New York: Simon & Schuster, 1993.

Gottman, John. *Why Marriages Fail: And How You Can Make Yours Last.* New York: Fireside, 1994.

———. *The Relationship Cure: A 5 Step Guide to Strengthening Your Marriage, Family, and Friendships.* New York: Three Rivers Press, 2001.

Greeley, Andrew M. *Sex: The Catholic Experience.* Allen, TX: Tabor Publishing, 1994.

Gurian, Michael. *The Wonder of Boys: What Parents, Mentors, and Educators Can Do to Shape Boys into Exceptional Men.* New York: Tarcher/Putnam, 1996.

Harris, Thomas A. *I'm OK—You're OK: A Practical Guide to Transactional Analysis.* New York: Harper & Row, 1969.

Hendrix, Harville. *Getting the Love You Want: A Guide for Couples.* New York: Henry Holt and Company, 1988.

Hoistad, Jan. *Big Picture Partnering: 16 Weeks to a Rock Solid Relationship.* Minneapolis: Twofold Publications, 2004.

Ivey, E. Allen, et al. *Counseling and Psychotherapy A Multicultural Perspective,* 4th ed. Boston: Allyn and Bacon, 1980.

Kramer, H. Charles. *Becoming a Family Therapist: Developing an Integrated Approach to Working with Families.* New York: Human Sciences Press, 1980.

Love, Patricia. *The Emotional Incest Syndrome: What to Do When a Parent's Love Rules Your Life.* New York: Bantam, 1991.

Maltz, Wendy. *The Sexual Healing Journey.* New York: HarperCollins, 1991, 2001 (rev. ed).

Mundis, Jerrold. *How to Get Out of Debt, Stay Out of Debt, and Live Prosperously.* New York: Bantam, 2003.

Myss, Caroline. *Anatomy of the Spirit: The Seven Stages of Power and Healing.* New York: Random House, 1996.

Pipher, Mary. *The Shelter of Each Other: Rebuilding Our Families.* New York: G.P. Putnam's Sons, 1996.

Rossi, Ernest Lawrence. *The Psychology of Mind Body Healing.* New York: Norton, 1986.

Schaef, Anne Wilson. *When Society Becomes an Addict.* New York: HarperCollins, 1988.

Twelve Step Recovery Programs

Adult Children of Alcoholics (ACA and ACOA)	www.adultchildren.org
Al-Anon and Alateen	www.al-anon.alateen.org
Alcoholics Anonymous (AA)	www.alcoholics-anonymous.org
Co-dependents Anonymous (CoDA)	www.codependents.org
Debtors Anonymous (DA)	www.debtorsanonymous.org
Gamblers Anonymous (GA)	www.gamblersanonymous.org
Narcotics Anonymous (NA)	www.na.org
Recovering Couples Anonymous (RCA)	www.recovering-couples.org
Sexaholics Anonymous (SA)	www.sa.org
Survivors of Incest Anonymous	www.siawso.org

Conflict Resolution and Mediation

Center for Nonviolent Communication	www.cnvc.org
Institute of Integrated Healing Arts	615-383-4449

Meditation CD

Woodel, Norm. *Six 11 Minute Attitude Adjustments,* available at www.voxershorts.com

Index

About the Author

Mary Faulkner makes her home on the banks of the South Harpeth River just outside of Nashville. She holds a master's degree in religious education and has published books and articles on the subject of religion, spirituality, and recovery—including *The Easy Does It Dating Guide* and *The Complete Idiot's Guide to Understanding Catholicism*. She has a counseling practice, teaches, holds workshops and retreats, and at other times can be found sitting and watching the river go by. Mary has three grown children and four grandchildren.

Hazelden Publishing and Educational Services is a division of the Hazelden Foundation, a not-for-profit organization. Since 1949, Hazelden has been a leader in promoting the dignity and treatment of people afflicted with the disease of chemical dependency.

The mission of the foundation is to improve the quality of life for individuals, families, and communities by providing a national continuum of information, education, and recovery services that are widely accessible; to advance the field through research and training; and to improve our quality and effectiveness through continuous improvement and innovation.

Stemming from that, the mission of this division is to provide quality information and support to people wherever they may be in their personal journey—from education and early intervention, through treatment and recovery, to personal and spiritual growth.

Although our treatment programs do not necessarily use everything Hazelden publishes, our bibliotherapeutic materials support our mission and the Twelve Step philosophy upon which it is based. We encourage your comments and feedback.

The headquarters of the Hazelden Foundation are in Center City, Minnesota. Additional treatment facilities are located in Chicago, Illinois; Newberg, Oregon; New York, New York; Plymouth, Minnesota; and St. Paul, Minnesota. At these sites, we provide a continuum of care for men and women of all ages. Our Plymouth facility is designed specifically for youth and families.

For more information on Hazelden, please call **1-800-257-7800.** Or you may access our World Wide Web site on the Internet at **www.hazelden.org.**

Other titles that may interest you

Easy Does It Dating Guide: For People in Recovery
Mary Faulkner
Sometimes humorous, always honest, this guide addresses dating issues often experienced by people in recovery from addiction. How much information do we share about our past? Should we date others in recovery? What about attraction to a problem drinker or drug user? Mary Faulkner offers practical, wise guidelines and exercises for exploring self and relationships.
Softcover, 232 pp.
Order No. 2143

Fearless Relationships: Simple Rules for Lifelong Contentment
Karen Casey
Drawing from her own life experiences and lessons learned the hard way, Karen Casey offers wise counsel about what helps and what hinders relationships. Her insights are at once familiar and revealing, reminding us of simple truths we need to rediscover for ourselves again and again.
Softcover, 152 pp.
Order No. 1998

Codependent No More: How to Stop Controlling Others and Start Caring for Yourself
Melody Beattie
With instructive real-life stories, personal reflections, exercises, and self-tests, this modern classic is a straightforward map through the otherwise tangled world of codependent relationships.
Softcover, 264 pp.
Order No. 5014

Hazelden books are available at fine bookstores everywhere. To order directly from Hazelden, call 1-800-328-9000 or visit www.hazelden.org/bookstore.